T0065246

I PRIED OPEN
WALL STREET
IN 1962

Other Books by the Author

Don't Get Mad, Get Rich

Live a Purposeful and Meaningful Life

I PRIED OPEN WALL STREET IN 1962

Overcoming Barriers, Hurdles and Obstacles

A Memoir

WINSTON E. ALLEN, Ph.D.

iUniverse

I PRIED OPEN WALL STREET IN 1962
OVERCOMING BARRIERS, HURDLES
AND OBSTACLES A MEMOIR

iUniverse books may be ordered through booksellers or by contacting:

iUniverse
1663 Liberty Drive
Bloomington, IN 47403
www.iuniverse.com
844-349-9409

Because of the dynamic nature of the Internet, any web addresses or links contained in this book may have changed since publication and may no longer be valid. The views expressed in this work are solely those of the author and do not necessarily reflect the views of the publisher, and the publisher hereby disclaims any responsibility for them.

Any people depicted in stock imagery provided by Getty Images are models, and such images are being used for illustrative purposes only. Certain stock imagery © Getty Images.

ISBN: 978-1-6632-2053-0 (sc)
ISBN: 978-1-6632-2546-7 (hc)
ISBN: 978-1-6632-2052-3 (e)

Library of Congress Control Number: 2021906606

Print information available on the last page.

iUniverse rev. date: 08/25/2021

Contents

Part IV. Civil Rights Movement, 1920-1968

Part V. Giving Back, 1950-Present

Part VI. Rotary Work and Other Projects

Acknowledgments

I want to thank and acknowledge two special people in my life who worked directly with me to make this book possible. This book could not have been written without the support and loving assistance of my wife, Ruby Allen and my son Vaughn Allen for their review, for their comments, and for their invaluable support in so many ways. They made this book possible by keeping my life calm, peaceful and happy.

I am deeply indebted to those individuals who, over the years, have shared their knowledge with me and provided me with invaluable insights. My passion for books has rewarded me with a deeper understanding and fresh thinking. The words of Ralph Ellison and James Baldwin, noted black authors from years ago, taught, inspired and motivated me in the early 1950s. Those two outspoken champions from our past propelled me forward.

Introduction

I fostered success by overcoming barriers, hurdles and obstacles that had been put in place from the beginning of Wall Street. On December 2, 1962 I was able to open the first black-owned Wall Street firm, Creative Investor Services Inc. by prying open the doors to Wall Street that were slammed shut. I also demonstrated how to succeed on Wall Street during a very difficult time in our country's history without being white.

This meant my firm brought newly ascendant minorities into my business with two heralded courses I devised that enabled them to pass a difficult NASD exam, along with another marketing course that resulted in their disproving the myth that there was no capital in the black community for investing. In those circles I became known as the "Black Moses" of Wall Street.

The idea of providing the black community with straight talk was novel in 1964 when I pitched how to profit on Wall Street and in the United States (U.S.), with confidence in a number of personally sponsored seminars on how to be profitable in Wall Street and in the U.S. I saw the goal as an equal chance to succeed rather than special treatment. I said, *"We don't guarantee success. We want the opportunity to earn it."*

This book is an opportunity to remember some rarely presented aspects of U.S. history, including the obstacles faced by outsiders on Wall Street, the civil rights and post–civil rights impact on upward mobility, and the impact I have made on philanthropy and community service and development.

PART I

My Developmental Years, 1946-1961

Chapter 1

My First Experience in the South, 1946

It was the day of my long-anticipated train ride to Miami, Florida, from New York City, and I saw myself being rushed aboard a train, the Silver Meter Express. My mother and father led by a sleeping car porter, ushered me into a sleeping car compartment and quickly shut the door. The porter said, "Welcome aboard. You will get all your meals brought to you, but you will not be permitted to leave this compartment with its bathroom and shower, until we get to the last station in Miami." He added, "I am required to lock the door from the outside—for the entire trip. All your meals will be brought to you by the porters."

As a wide-eyed, innocent thirteen-year-old boy in 1946, I embarked on a train ride from New York City through the Deep South, with the ultimate destination of Jamaica in the Caribbean, to spend my summer vacation on a campaign trip with my uncle E. V. Allen for his sixth term as a prominent member of the Jamaican House of Representatives. The train was quickly filling up, and there was no time to talk. No one told me why I was in a locked car, and everything was happening so fast. I had no idea why I was going to be stuck in this compartment for the entire trip. I thought maybe it was because I was traveling alone or underage.

I did not know it at the time, but later I learned that specific arrangements had been made by my parents with the sleeping car porters in New York City to circumvent the Jim Crow segregation laws that prohibited black people from being in a sleeping car compartment. Those laws were strictly enforced in southern states. Later 1 came to learn how dire the consequences could have been for me as I traveled through eight segregated states. I didn't know it then, but I was about to have a transformative experience. It was from this trip that I first got a peek at some of the barriers, hurdles and obstacles that would be with me for my entire life.

After the train rolled out of Pennsylvania Station, I watched people enter and leave the train in New York, New Jersey and Pennsylvania. I was looking forward to a fun trip as I peered out the window. A few hours later, I heard an announcement over the loudspeaker "In fifteen minutes we will be arriving in Washington, D.C. Collect all suitcases and prepare to depart." No one I knew had ever been to Washington, D.C.

As the train slowly pulled into the dark, huge, underground Union Station, I was astounded. The station lit up for me when I first saw the blaring WHITES ONLY and COLORED signs at every waiting room, restroom and water fountain. Everything suddenly changed. I was shocked. There, through my young eyes, were the startling huge, blazing signs. I had no one in my compartment to talk to, so I talked to myself. I knew that something had just changed in my understanding when the capital of my country saw me as needing to be separated.

These signs continued at each station as the train moved through Delaware, Virginia, Maryland, North Carolina, South Carolina, Georgia and Florida. I was aghast. Those ever-present "WHITES ONLY and COLORED" signs at every water fountain, every waiting room and every restroom. Everyone was obeying the signs without any hesitation or reluctance. I had never seen such signs before. I wondered, who put those signs there? Why are they being obeyed? I watched in disbelief.

Everyone knew exactly what to do and where to go. Whites went to the doors with signs reading "WHITES ONLY," and BLACKS went to the doors with signs stating "COLORED." That was my first time experiencing outright segregation. I could not believe what I was seeing. I thought, Washington is the nation's capital. It can't be.

At thirteen years old, this was all new to me. The feeling of shock was immediate, and it quickly turned to resentment and outrage at what I was seeing. Most of the night, I watched each station in Delaware, Virginia, Maryland, North Carolina, South Carolina, Georgia and Florida, in both small towns and large cities. I waited to see if they all had the same signs. As the train rolled into each station, black kids younger than five years of age in ragged clothes were waiting for the train so they could pick up coins that were thrown at them from white passengers getting on and off the train as they helped the passengers with their bags. Moreover, all the blacks were poor, or so it appeared to me. As I later came to learn, Jim Crow, segregation and poverty had all contributed to it.

The kids knew just where to stand to be at the right place to grab the bags from the passengers and drop them at the WHITES ONLY door. They quickly grabbed the coins that were thrown at them and ran back to find other passengers waiting down the track. Little did I know that everything I was watching was based on rigidly enforced Jim Crow in all the towns, cities and states I was passing through with severe police and mob action waiting to seize a black violator for the slightest deviation from the rules. I would not have felt so safe after seeing those signs, even locked in my compartment, had I known what the consequences could have been. From my compartment window, the contrast was striking between this and anything I had ever seen before. I felt horrified by it. It was as if I was in a strange country. Not only was I mystified, but I was completely puzzled. I felt whiplashed. My eyes had seen so much, and what I had not seen explicitly became known to me implicitly.

When I arrived in Jamaica and told them what I had seen, I was amazed that they knew in Jamaica what I had seen for the first time in the U.S. I kept remembering the looks of disdain and indifference on the faces of the passengers as the kids groveled for the coins that were thrown at them. It was like what I had seen on my trips to the zoo as the warden tossed scraps of food at the animals, the difference being that there was no look of disdain as they did so.

Jamaica was a blessing. Large crowds of people, almost all black with some whites, filled the campaign waiting areas both as we drove by and at each stop. There was adoration for my uncle E. V. Allen. Why were things so different? In Jamaica there were no WHITE and COLORED signs, no kids begging for coins in ragged clothes, and no racial separation of people. A great deal of reverence was expressed for a black man, my uncle, who was their representative in the Jamaican Congress.

Back from Jamaica on the train from Miami to New York at the end of the summer, I watched closely at each station. I remember the resolve I had developed because of the images that I saw, and the disdain that was shown by many of the passengers for the black kids on the whole. They were treated with indifference. I felt horrified by what I was again seeing. I vowed I would never allow myself to

4

be treated that way. In later years I have gone back over my trip at thirteen years old to relive how it affected the person that I became, an overachieving, enterprising person who endures to this day. I also quickly developed into a street-smart kid.

Although I never experienced Jim Crow firsthand, I did experience the widespread effects of segregation that prevailed everywhere in the U.S. and what I believed to be racial animosities on numerous occasions. Jim Crow and terrorizing invariably does long lasting injuries to the inner soul of a black person. Had I grown up in an oppressive Jim Crow environment I would not have developed into who I have become; competitive, resourceful and fearless.

After the anger stage I went through, I reflected on what I had seen from the train window and my feelings turned to resourcefulness, enterprise and independence. That train ride and summer trip changed my attitude and behavior and shaped my vision of my future self. I decided to immediately increase my knowledge of conditions under Jim Crow, segregation and poverty that I had observed. I learned what life was like for powerless black people throughout the South, and I sought answers as to how black people endured what I had gotten a taste of.

I enjoyed reading because when I did so, I learned so much I did not know. I read every book I could find on what is now known as ethnic studies, sometimes more than once: Ralph Ellison's The Invisible Man, James Baldwin's The Fire Next Time, Richard Wright's Native Son, and as soon as it came out, The Autobiography of Malcolm X, whose mother incidentally was born and raised in the island of Grenada where my mother grew up. Maybe this is part of the reason why his ideas and mine were so much in sync.

5

Winston E. Allen, Ph.D.

Harlem had been the headquarters of Garvey's Universal Negro Improvement Association and of the African Communities League of the World, the largest mass black movement of the time. My interest had started with my witnessing the demanded servile behavior that had been forced on blacks in the South by self-serving whites. Seeing the effects in people who had lived to imbibe institutionalized racism had a profound effect upon me as I could view things I came in contact through a different lens.

Chapter 2
Harlem, 1898–1960

Between 1898 and 1900 wealthy whites from lower Manhattan were attracted to the new residential haven of Harlem. They enjoyed the deluxe life in Harlem until the real estate bust came with a blast in 1904 because of the overbuilding that had occurred. Speculators sadly realized afterward that too many buildings had been constructed at one time, leading to many vacancies and thousands of unoccupied apartments.

Threatened by financial ruin, owners rented their deluxe apartments to black families and collected the traditionally higher rents that blacks had been conditioned to pay because of their limited chances of finding desirable housing. For the first time in New York City's history, blacks had access to decent housing. In the past, there had been no such opportunity anywhere in the U.S. Now blacks in Harlem as a whole were better housed than in any other part of the U.S.

Of all the black neighborhoods in the U.S., Harlem, where I grew up, was unique. I later learned that when it was first constructed, Harlem was a symbol of elegance and distinction; its streets and avenues were broad, well paved and tree lined. It was no longer necessary for black people to live in small, dingy, stuffy tenements once blacks were able to move into Harlem, said an editorial in the Amsterdam News. Harlem, by contrast, was heaven. Harlem was not merely the largest black community in the world but was the first concentration in history that attracted so many diverse elements of black life. Harlem was diverse because it had attracted blacks from the Caribbean, the South and Africa.

My grandmother

Mother and Father

Harlem Residence   Me at Four

My mother and father were both immigrants who came through Ellis Island. My mother came from the Caribbean islands of Grenada in 1923, and my father came from Jamaica in 1929, two islands that were about 1200 miles apart. My mother's father was Superintendent of Schools for the island of Grenada, and my father's brother was a member of the House of Representatives for Jamaica. My mother had a luxurious upbringing, and my father too, had a comfortable life in Jamaica with a brother, E. V. Allen, who served seven terms in the Jamaican Congress. They believed in education and striving for excellence in anything that they did. They came to the U.S. at a most difficult time for blacks in the U.S. When I was growing up, what they did was to imbue me with an inner sense of self-confidence.

My parents, having met through mutual friends soon after they'd arrived in the U.S., married and settled in an apartment on 113th Street and St. Nicholas Avenue, three blocks from the northern boundary of Central Park. Harlem, as our family knew it, was only an example of the general development of large communities in many U.S. cities in the years immediately before and following World War I. The black sections of Harlem remained and expanded.

Harlem's history can be defined as a series of economic boom-and-bust cycles. By 1930 black Harlem had reached its southern limit, of 110th Street, the northern boundary of Central Park, which is where I lived proudly. Its population was then approximately two hundred thousand. Harlem was the first concentration in history of so many diverse elements of black life. In 1920, Harlem was developing into a popular black neighborhood among New York City's African Americans. At the time, 90 percent of the black population in the U.S. lived in the South, most of them in rural areas.

From 1915 to 1970, the exodus of six million blacks from Jim Crow, lynching and oppression in the South changed the face of the U.S. If blacks in slum sections of New York thought that they had it bad escaping the slums of mid-town Manhattan to Harlem, the Southern blacks had it far worse, contending with severe poverty, discriminatory Jim Crow laws and frequent lynching to destination cities such as Chicago and New York.

To me, the Harlem I lived in as a child was just plain old Harlem, a bunch of varied neighborhoods where many of the residents, such as my family, were focused on education, self-improvement and community uplifting as they maintained a positive attitude about life. A few Harlem residents whom we became familiar with were fairly well-off. Some others had fallen on hard times, and most were just trying to make a decent living and raise a family.

I believed that where I lived was a special place, and I felt very fortunate to grow up surrounded by supportive family and friends. The people I knew had a remarkable ability to take the barest shreds of opportunity and in spite of unfortunate circumstances and meager resources at their disposal, they strived to live purposeful and meaningful lives. Black sections mushroomed, resulting in overcrowding in urban areas of Harlem and in cities such as Baltimore, Chicago, Boston, Philadelphia and Washington, D.C.

We lived three blocks from Central Park with its huge lake, good for rowing and fishing. There were woods and bicycle paths. In comparison, times were tough for many we knew who had difficulty finding and keeping a job during the Great Depression. Though my family had modest means, we never had impoverished dreams.

My parents planted seeds in me to bear fruit and for success. My parents encouraged me to listen to classical music, jazz, watch ballet and visit art museums. It is not surprising, therefore, that I ended up at a music and art high school, although I knew from the start that I was not going in the direction of a career in music.

My father fortunately landed a good job at Rockefeller Center as a uniform elevator operator during these years. Just before that job, he was the superintendent of a six-story building with artists who painted there in their studios in a well-known building, the Del

Mar Studios, located at Fifty-Seventh Street and Eighth Avenue in Manhattan. When the building was sold after my father had been there six years and the art studios were closing, the artists got my father his new job at Rockefeller Center, not an easy thing to do for a black man at that time. During his entire tenure at Rockefeller Center my father never missed a day of work. He often came home with complementary tickets for special events in the city. We enjoyed trips to Radio City, Madison Square Garden and the circus, along with passes for ice-skating in the rink at Rockefeller.

My mother, skilled as a dressmaker, felt fortunate to have landed a job as a finisher at Sam Friedlander's Garment Factory on Thirty-Seventh Street and Seventh Avenue. Since both my parents were working full time, my mother sponsored my aunt to come over from Grenada and live with us. My aunt accepted. She took care of the household chores while my parents worked. Throughout my stay at apartment 4A at 60 St. Nicholas Avenue, for twenty-five years, the rent for our seven-room apartment was fifty-three dollars a month.

Black skill development, economic growth and the civil rights movement all contributed to the surfacing of a larger black middle class. The civil rights movement helped to remove some barriers to higher education. As opportunities for black Americans expanded, blacks began to take advantage of the new possibilities. Home ownership was crucial in the rise of the black middle class, including the movement of African Americans to the suburbs, which often resulted in better educational opportunities.

Although most of the country did not understand it, there was a serious problem percolating around the race issue within the many black segregated urban areas. Central to that fact was that most of these segregated communities were controlled by non-black outsiders. As blacks engaged in the fight to gain control of their communities, they were met with strong resistance. There was a raging battle for opportunities by blacks and an awareness that desegregation was improbable. In neighborhoods within Harlem, there had been much in the historical background of black people that had made survival difficult. This history had produced a people able to be knocked down by life circumstances and come back again and again.

A few individual blacks at that time were able to take advantage of minimal opportunities and convert them into some achievements. The reason for the success of some black people was no different from anyone else. Hard work, perseverance, determination, entrepreneurship and the drive to be successful. Unfortunately, the biggest drawback facing blacks the color of their skin. They succeeded in the face of overwhelming odds, which is remarkable. It has now been replicated by many other individuals. From time to time, opportunities have opened up in various levels of society that have enabled a most resilient people to survive and, in a slowly growing number of cases, to prosper.

In the 1930s Harlem was hit hard by the Great Depression and the subsequent job losses following the crash of October 1929. In the early 1930s, more than half the residents of Harlem were out of work, and their employment prospects stayed low for decades, wiping out the limited wealth of many residents who had lost their jobs and their homes. Many businesses closed, and some areas became undesirable. In the epic *The Warmth of Other Suns*, Pulitzer prize-winning author Isabel Wilkerson chronicles one of the great

13

untold stories of U.S. history: the decades-long migration of six million black citizens who fled the Jim Crow South for northern and western cities in search of better lives. From 1915 to 1970, this exodus of six million people from the South changed the face of the U.S., exacerbating the already overcrowded conditions in housing and public schools, in the face of horrid unemployment in neighborhoods like Harlem. In most cases, segregated schools were at best "separate but unequal." Segregated housing invariably resulted in segregated schools in the North, and in the 1940s and 1950s, Harlem schools were poorly funded, under resourced and inadequately staffed. In my experience, schools were almost as segregated in the North as in the South.

Public School (PS) 10 was my district elementary school assigned by the New York City Board of Education. Segregated black "redlined" housing neighborhoods often had low-performing schools. In the 1930s, government surveyors graded neighborhoods in 239 cities, color-coding them green for "best," blue for "still desirable," yellow for "definitely declining," and red for "hazardous." The redlined areas were the ones local lenders discounted as credit risks, in large part because of the residents' racial and ethnic demographics.

My assigned elementary school, which I walked to each day on 117th Street and St. Nicholas Avenue, was a low-performing school. Once, in frustration, my mother took off the morning from her job to meet with my third-grade teacher and asked her why there appeared to be no arithmetic being taught to students. My teacher matter-of-factly responded with an answer that I remember to this day: "Mrs. Allen, laboring jobs, which these kids may get if they are lucky, do not require arithmetic, so why burden them with subjects they will never need?" That curt, brief and didactic meeting resulted in my mother's choosing to homeschool me each evening when she came home from work.

From the 1930s, racial discrimination in housing mortgage lending shaped the demographic and wealth patterns of American neighborhoods. With three out of four neighborhoods redlined for black children on government maps, the economic struggle for blacks continued unabated. Loans in these neighborhoods were unavailable or very expensive, making it extremely difficult for low-income minorities to buy homes and setting the stage for the country's persistent and ever-growing racial wealth gap.

On a personal quest for information, I discovered that the basis for part of the inequitable schooling, overloading, inadequate funding and educational benefits among schools was that school districts relied on local property taxes as their primary source of funding. Thus, wealthier districts had more resources to draw from than did the schools in low-income communities. Resources were unevenly distributed, and many schools that served students with greater needs received fewer resources. Allocations at the individual school level were largely low because of lack of transparency and understanding of the budget process at the local level. The schools open to me in Harlem were no exception, being understaffed, underfunded and underperforming. This is cited in Linda Darling-Hammond's Sunday, March 1, 1998, article from Brookings: "Unequal Opportunity: Race and Education."

Harlem, on the other hand, was known as the cultural and intellectual hub of black America in the 1920s and 1930s and was the focus of the Harlem Renaissance, an outpouring of artistic works without precedent in the American black community. Though Harlem's musicians and actors, including Paul Robeson and Marian Anderson, are particularly well remembered, a number of writers of poetry, essays and criticism also emerged: Claude McKay, Langston Hughes, Countee Cullen, James Weldon Johnson, James Baldwin and Walter White.

Chapter 3
My Early Years, 1940–1980

My folks, although somewhat fearless, were smart in wanting me to experience firsthand the world as it was. But in the summer of 1946, some might say that they had gone too far, putting a young black boy on a train going from New York City through the Deep South with only a handshake guarantee that the train's sleeping car porters would be able to protect me, with gratuities to help ensure this would happen. Nonetheless, the experience gave me what I had no other way of visualizing.

I am able to appreciate the insight it gave me. If these were my feelings in only a few days, I wonder what crippling everlasting effect was implanted in the minds of children and adults who were forced to experience terrorism, degradation and humiliation daily all throughout their lives. That story has yet to be told. If anything, it energized my belief that one must not be unprepared as a minority. It is a good thing that I had my guard up because I was about to face some challenges, in my new school in a middle class out of district school, but I stood my ground, and my adversaries backed off.

My next assigned school, James Fenimore Cooper Junior High School, in East Harlem on 120th Street, for students living in our redlined neighborhood in Harlem, was another low-performing school in the 1940s. My mother was so incensed with the local school's indifference to educating the students in this district that she had my address transferred to a friend's address in the district.

My mother had schemed and, using a friend's address in a wealthy Manhattan school district, had gotten me into a new school, Joan of Arc Junior High School, on West End Avenue and 93rd Street with mostly white kids and teachers often with expressions of white superiority. I was ready for that, although I had little to combat it with, except higher level work than was expected. This was how I developed my drive to be as good as or better than my competition.

This junior high school reflected the neighborhood's demographics and had an almost all-white student body. The neighborhood consisted of high-rise doorman buildings on the avenues and brownstone buildings on the side streets. I was one of a few black students in the school of over twelve hundred students. This ten-story school could have benefited from some diversification.

My next school, two years later, was the highly rated High School of Music and Art (M&A), popularly known as the "Castle on the Hill," because it is perched on a hill in Manhattan overlooking the city. It all began for me when I took and passed the examination for this prestigious public school. I took the entrance examination for admission as a music student and was asked to demonstrate skill in playing two piano selections and answering questions about them. Things evidently went well because a few days later I received an acceptance in the mail to this four-year high school. I realized that the many years of practicing the piano had paid off.

Music and Art High School

The High School of M&A was founded during the administration of Mayor Fiorello H. LaGuardia in 1936, during the Depression. LaGuardia described it as his most hopeful accomplishment. As the mayor of New York City, he wanted to establish a public school in which students could hone their talents in music and art. It was a magnet school, meant to draw talented and aspiring students from all five boroughs.

M&A was a next step because music had been a part of my life starting when I was about five years old and we got a roller player piano in our apartment that magically played all the familiar tunes. Soon after that, my family bought an upright piano, and I was able to start with lessons, first with my mother teaching me and soon after with Ms. Lowe, who was my first formal piano teacher.

The prestigious M&A was not too far from where we lived in Harlem, just two subway stations away. It was located at 135th Street and St Nicholas Terrace. This type of school became a forerunner of today's magnet schools. It featured a specialized music and art curriculum and drew students from all over the city. Some students traveled more than an hour and a half from outlying boroughs in Brooklyn and Staten Island to get to the school.

For me there are two things that stand out about M&A. First, we were a class act of selected students from all over the city. Second, while 99 percent of U.S. high schools marched to their graduation and other assemblies to the strains of "Pomp and Circumstance," we marched accompanied by the melodious *Ouvertüre to Die Meistersinger*. It was well chosen, and I felt privileged to be in the senior chorus, performing many times at gala events. Secondly, what other class petitioned the Board of Education to teach them higher mathematics?

In our senior year, we performed Beethoven's Ninth for the senior concert with the senior orchestra and chorus. This composition moves me to this day, more than any other piece of music, perhaps because I am conscious of the composer's profound deafness. He only heard the music in his mind's ear. Near the end, the full chorus and orchestra hits a minor chord and holds it for a full measure. The moment is sublime. My reaction is still visceral with tears in my eyes and a catch in my throat. What a privilege it was to be a part of this. I spent my four years at this specialized high school, taking Advanced Placement academic courses. I thank all who made it possible for me to go to a great school, M&A.

After graduation I applied to college and opted to go to New York University (NYU) Washington Square College of Arts and Sciences because of its great reputation and because I enjoyed being in Greenwich Village. The Village had a heavy concentration of musicians, artists, writers and other hardworking people with varied interests and lifestyles. Where else would you find a pianist who rolls his grand piano out to Washington Square Park on sunny days to practice and to entertain the NYU students and other park visitors but Greenwich Village adjacent to NYU? That was unique.

Pianist who rolled out his grand piano to play to the crowd

Washington Square Park Pianist

I made a good choice in selecting NYU. I have never forgotten the time that I spent at NYU's Washington Square College. Although it was a large school in terms of size, it was a small school in its individual features. I majored in Economics and history as a Liberal Arts, pre-med student. I am also reminded of the good times and friendships that were formed on the trips a group of us took each spring on our drives to the Penn Relays.

I selected the pre-med program partially because it was the most challenging liberal arts course of study at the time with a dose of science, literatures and humanities. A major feature of this program for me was that it required a huge amount of discipline, which I wanted at the time. I needed to assure myself that I could handle one of the most strenuous programs an undergraduate could take at NYU. I also took on an after-school job at the NYU bookstore, because I love books and I had the opportunity to meet many students from various disciplines.

By the time I graduated in 1955, I was assured that applying to medical school was not my career goal. NYU Law School was another possibility for graduate school. The NYU Law School was only two blocks away from the undergraduate school that I had attended. I also applied and was admitted to Columbia University Law School, but I chose NYU Law School an easier commute.

I knew what I did not want to do, but I did not know what I wanted to do on a long-term basis. I later discovered that left-brain types were more in tune with the day-to-day examination of legal cases than a right-brain type like me, who is stimulated by searching out novel ways of solving problems and coming up with new ideas. With a better perception of my personality type back then, I could have sought out a field that was more in tune with an intuitive type of person. The takeaway from this experience is that a person is far better off with that knowledge when making life-long decisions. After a successful first year at law school dealing with contracts and torts, I decided to leave NYU Law School in May.

Early in September, I saw a newspaper ad that reported a shortage of New York City teachers at the beginning of the 1956 school year.

22

While I had not considered teaching as a career in the past, I needed a job, so I went to the Board of Education, at 110 Livingston Street, Brooklyn, one morning and asked the attendant what I needed to do to get on a substitute teaching list. When I showed the attendant my NYU undergraduate and NYU Law School résumé, I was whisked straightaway to the office of Dr. Lillian Rashkis. After a brief interview, Dr. Rashkis told me that she wanted me to take a teaching exam that afternoon to assess my qualifications.

I evidently passed, because then Dr. Rashkis told me that instead of putting me on a list for substitute teaching, she was offering me a full-time regular assignment as a teacher at Public School (PS) 611 beginning the next morning at 7:30. She told me the school was located at 138 Street and Paul Avenue in the Bronx and that the principal was Francis J. Jones. Getting a full-time job and earning a regular salary, rather than waiting for a possible telephone call, was a welcome surprise.

Dr. Rashkis was certainly didactic, but the speed of her decision gave me pause, I had no knowledge of what a 600 school was, and I knew nothing of the student body. I found the school the next morning in a section of the South Bronx commonly known as "Fort Apache" because of the active gangs in the neighborhood.

The next day when I met Francis J. Jones, the principal, he greeted me, saying, "I'm relieved that the Board of Education finally found a regular teacher to fill a vacant classroom spot. I am going to take you down to the entrance and show you what you will be doing when the boys come through the front door each morning. They line up outside. When the doors open and they enter one by one, you will search them for contraband, usually knives and zip-guns.

23

You will put those items in a box and bring them to my office. Good luck!" I never saw the principal again, except casually, for weeks and sometimes months.

PS 611 housed an all-boys' school with students in their late teens. It was a three-floor brick building with about twenty classrooms. The classes were small in size, so with only about ten students on any given day, there was plenty of room. I gave my students the freedom of sitting wherever they liked, as long as they were not disruptive. I had many books and magazines for their reading pleasure during their free period, when I met with individual students to talk with me about whatever they wanted to talk with me about.

The 600 schools in New York City were designed to educate emotionally disturbed and socially maladjusted children. I found that my students related well and were not difficult to handle once they felt comfortable with me. Students were recommended to a special school (600 school) by their regular schoolteachers once it was clear that they would continue to disturb the learning process for the other students in regular classes. By the 1970s, the 600 schools paved the way to what came to be known as District 75, which serves a disproportionate number of black and Hispanic students who were classified as emotionally disturbed and who had been removed from their community schools.

I was able to give students individual attention and work with them one-on-one, which was a new experience for them and for me. They seemed to like it. All the other teachers were white. The kids were black, Hispanic, and white and the principal, Francis Jones, was white. I was the only black teacher the school had ever had.

I was told by the principal that my students were likely to be difficult and volatile, but despite the students being characterized as emotionally disturbed, some with rap sheets and arrest records, they turned out to be very amenable after I had established a trusting relationship with them. They remained with me, their homeroom teacher, for the entire school day with the exception of two industrial arts classes each week.

From time to time, I assigned my class some questions to answer after reading some books that I had given them. I then discussed with other students, while they were occupied, a subject of their choosing. They decided whatever they wanted to talk to me about. We explored many areas of each student's personal and family life and their future plans. That was a bonding mechanism. From these conversations, I learned a great deal about the lives of my students. I understood their concerns about their personal safety in their neighborhoods. This was always a popular session. They explained in detail their reasons for joining street gangs and arming themselves with zip guns to survive.

These discussions with my students aroused in me an interest to talk to people about their inner feelings and their lives. To further pursue this end, I enrolled in an after-school program in psychotherapy training that was very cogent and proved to be invaluable in many of my future positions. I considered becoming a therapist for a while after completing the three-year course. I finally decided that I would continue in the teaching field until I found my niche.

One notion that propelled me toward my own business and being my own boss was the realization that so many fields, such as teaching, did not provide one with the power to influence the decisions that were being made by a distant Board of Education. I needed to have a

25

decision-making role in any field I would choose. I quietly resolved that I needed to go into business on my own.

Motivating the kids in my class was the key to keeping them engaged and disciplined. There was no required curriculum that I needed to follow, so I met with each student daily and learned their concerns and interests. I discovered through these talks that almost all of them had a common interest: playing a musical instrument. I decided to start a small band. When I asked them how we were going to get instruments, they all said in a chorus, "Don't worry, Teach. We'll get instruments!"

Within days, we had a drum set, a trumpet and a saxophone. As the weeks went by, my students brought more instruments to school, and soon after they began playing recognizable tunes. The boys looked forward to our jam sessions. Since they didn't read music, I had them improvise on popular tunes they knew. Our regular jam sessions could be heard outside my classroom, livening up the school. The band's popularity grew. Attending the High School of M&A and playing the piano had given me the skills to help my students improvise and keep the band in tune.

Principal Jones publicized to the principals of the other 600 schools that PS 611 had developed the first orchestra in the 600-school system. Principal Jones encouraged me to continue the band and expand on it. He was enamored by the idea that he had a singularly unique addition to his school, for which he was able to gain prestige for PS 611 through the first ever musical band, which he publicized as an orchestra.

Toward the end of my first-year teaching position at PS 611, I decided that if I was going to stay in the teaching field for a while longer, I would be wise to take the high school teaching exam in social studies so that I could teach Economics. I passed the exam and was able to seek appointments to a high school.

Principal Jones then said to me, "I am going to help you locate a teaching position at a great high school, and I am making arrangements for you to be interviewed for a position at DeWitt Clinton High School in the Bronx. I have sent a strong recommendation to the principal, Walter Degnan, who is a personal friend of mine. He is planning to meet with you by the end of this week." We met and he offered me the position.

In June 1958, I left PS 611 in the Bronx after my interview with Principal Walter Degnan at DeWitt Clinton High School. In September 1958, the Board of Education officially assigned me to the school as a teacher of Economics, U.S. history and world history. Apparently, this was thrusting me down a road that was propelling me further into a teaching career.

There could not have been a more striking difference between PS 611 and DeWitt Clinton High School. The only common element was that both schools served boys only. One of these schools, PS 611, served primarily minority students who knew that they had been rejected by their regular school, their teachers and their principal. There were teachers at PS 611 whom I had never met in my two years there because we were all assigned to classes with little or no interaction. There were no assemblies for students and teachers to be in the same space and no free periods for teachers to get together to compare notes and experiences at PS 611. I did not know that in other schools there were assemblies, teachers with free periods and a principal seen interacting with teachers.

The other of these schools, DeWitt Clinton High School, served largely middleclass students who were enjoying their high school experience with the hope of going forward with their education upon graduation, mostly to college. Many students here were taking honors classes and being served by a college advisory department. DeWitt Clinton had consistently winning teams in all the sports of the city. The school had a record with both winning citywide teams and academics and a large Advanced Placement student body.

DeWitt Clinton opened its doors in 1897. In 1929, the school moved to a twenty-one-acre campus on Mosholu Parkway in the North Bronx, a middle-class neighborhood with parks and playgrounds. This high school procured a well-trained faculty of very devoted teachers. At one point in its history, it was so popular that there were twelve thousand students split into two sessions. During my teaching years at DeWitt Clinton, we had seven thousand boys in attendance and over two hundred teachers. The principal, Walter Degnan, a well-respected leader in both athletics and academics, was a popular figure in the school.

When I first started teaching at the high school level, as was true of all levels, I realized that the curriculum was prescribed by the Board of Education in New York City. All teachers were to rely on the established blueprint for direction in classrooms. This was particularly restrictive in social studies and in history classes because it limited a teacher's ability to bring specialized knowledge to the attention of students for their understanding and examination.

In my second year, however, I obtained approval from my Department Chairman to teach two honors classes for seniors called Ethnic Studies. One elective course that I taught was on the Harlem Renaissance. Students' readings centered on the biographies of intellectuals such as

W. E. B. DuBois, historian; Paul Robeson, athlete and world-famous opera singer and black history leader; and Langston Hughes, author and poet. To broaden my knowledge of black history, I researched several additional books on the subject that enhanced my teaching and my knowledge. The second course was a black cultural history course. Most DeWitt Clinton High School students were white and not apprised of black history. Also, I was asked to teach an adult education class in beginning piano in the evening at DeWitt Clinton's Night School.

During my second year at DeWitt Clinton High School, I formed the first school's Economics club for students with expectations of majoring in Economics in college. They welcomed the extracurricular field trips that I took them on, especially to Wall Street in downtown Manhattan and the Johnson and Johnson Corporation in New Brunswick, New Jersey. I enjoyed my teaching experiences but could not envision a thirty-five-year stay until retirement, as was customary for tenured teachers with a lifetime pension of 75 percent of their highest salary.

DeWitt Clinton High School economics club meeting wit
Winston Allen, ca. 1960.

Chapter 4

My Personal Experiences Overcoming Redlining

In 1966 I was looking for a home in lower Westchester and saw an ad for a house for sale in a town, Larchmont, Westchester that was known to be redlined. I decided to test the system. I called the broker and was told the house was available for showing if I could make it there within an hour. Saying I would be there, I went immediately. The owner was not at home. I liked the house, immediately I placed a deposit on it.

The next day I received a phone call from the broker stating that the seller was not going to sell her house to a black purchaser. The seller wanted the transaction rescinded even though the broker had cashed my check, closing the transaction. That was the beginning of another hurdle that based on previous experiences I was prepared to overcome. I was told by the broker that the seller was so enraged because she felt that her real estate firm, Sutton & Whittemore, should have known that she would never sell to a black purchaser. She also stated that the broker had violated her right to choose whom she did not want to sell to. The seller demanded that the broker cancel the sale.

The broker phoned me several times the next few days to tell me that the seller was putting a great deal of pressure on the Sutton & Whittemore firm to persuade them to rescind the contract. She wanted them to promise me an even better house in New Rochelle an adjacent racially diversified town and payment to rescind the sale. I told Sutton & Whittemore to clearly inform the seller that my answer was unequivocable. No pressure could result in my changing the purchase agreement that had been cemented with the cashing of my deposit check.

The seller, when she heard that, began corralling her neighbors in the town to arrange a mass campaign and meeting at one of her neighbor's house one evening that week to attempt to find ways to pressure me to change my position. I was invited to attend the meeting and I readily agreed to attend. I had been through other similar situations. I wanted to make it clear to everyone in the town, including the seller that my answer was No!

At the meeting I told everyone that I was not going to agree to any changes in the purchase contract, which required an early closing date with an immediate transfer of the property to me. After several speeches by the seller and her friends and no viable option was left to the seller, all vein attempts at intimidation failed to work and the meeting concluded. The contract specified a prompt closing which was adhered to.

I moved into the house with my family with generally unfriendly neighbors, with one family exception the Elders. When I later chose to sell the house, the selling price, initially $12,500 five years earlier when I purchased it, sold for $450,000.

This is an illustration of how, wealth-building takes place in the absence of red-redlining, racial covenants or racial zoning restrictions. Blacks are often denied the opportunity to accumulate capital when they sell their house because the market for their homes in black neighborhoods, are rarely able to experience multiple increases in value. This is an illustration of the barriers, hurdles and obstacles that can occur in a redlined neighborhood.

Despite some successes in helping blacks overcome barriers that denied them the opportunity for wealth-building many other problems still persisted. I personally focused on historically redlined residential communities. I made it a point to penetrate redlined communities whenever I was purchasing real estate. Although there were barriers, hurdles and obstacles, I persisted, and with tenacity I prevailed.

Chapter 5

Fulbright Scholarship in Paris, 1961

Wealth, assets and economic advantages were passed on from generation to succeeding generation and circumstance relegated blacks to a permanently dependent, noncompetitive status. Thus, I chose to pursue the study of Economics in pursuit of tools that could provide a minority with the means to propel themselves into a competitive position in a majority society. What came into my mind was the Fulbright scholarship for my analysis of the subject and I came to ponder a comparative study of wealthy and powerful minority groups.

Without any delay, I forwarded my application, my résumé, and my college records to the Fulbright Scholarship Office in Washington, along with my biography, references, recommendations and a project proposal for a specified economic curriculum. I thought my chances were slim because there were so many applicants.

The Fulbright Scholarship, a highly competitive merit-based grant for international educational fellowship for U.S. graduate students and professionals to study abroad for one academic year. It still remains one of the most prestigious award programs worldwide, operating in over one hundred fifty-five countries. The Fulbright Scholarship describes itself, in talks that I attended, as the U.S. governments flagship program for international educational exchange.

The Fulbright Program provided eight thousand grants annually to individuals to undertake graduate study, advanced research, university lecturing and classroom teaching and continues to be managed by the Institute of International Education and the U.S. Department of State's Bureau of Educational and Cultural Affairs. They sponsor the program with an annual appropriation from Congress. Those recommended for Fulbright grants have high academic achievement, a compelling project proposal and a statement of purpose, and have demonstrated leadership potential, flexibility and adaptability to interact successfully with the host community abroad.

After a lengthy and exhaustive process, I received an acceptance letter from the Secretary of State for an award in 1961, and I obtained a leave of absence from DeWitt Clinton High School to attend. It was a marvelous opportunity. I felt so fortunate because I was searching for an opportunity to travel and study abroad, only to apply for and be awarded a Fulbright Scholarship which granted me a fully paid scholarship to study at the Sorbonne in Paris, France, in 1961.

My program abroad was divided into three phases. The first phase was devoted to an academic program with morning lectures and afternoon discussions in Economics with the requirement that students must attend all classes. The second phase consisted of organized visits to points of historical significance in France; we visited Normandy, Brittany and the Loire Valley. The third phase provided time for personal travel at my discretion.

I pursued my scholarship days in Paris with eagerness and vigor. I was at the University of Paris in France, studying in my major field. In addition, the scholarship gave me a spectacular traveling opportunity, of which I took full advantage. My goal of postgraduate education and international travel from an apartment on the Left Bank of Paris on the rue des Écoles had been fulfilled.

It was beyond spectacular. I had such a great experience, like no other since, and I have a detailed memory of it to this day. Living in Paris in 1961 as my first European trip was a lot to absorb. Economics as my major was pointing me in a direction that would lead me from the theoretical to the practical, and I was thinking about how I could apply this new-found knowledge, data and perspective when I got back home to the harsh realities.

Fulbright Scholarship Classes

Fulbright Scholarship Classes

Each Friday after class, I was packed and ready to go to Gare du Nord, the main train station in Paris, and catch the next express train to a new country and city. My decision as to where I would go was based on the posted schedule for the overnight trains. I eliminated a hotel cost for Friday night and Sunday night at the end of the weekend. After the first night's travel, the train got me to a new country at dawn. I only needed to have a hotel for Saturday night and plan to be in class on Monday morning. My remaining time was free. I found myself in Rome, Munich, Geneva, Amsterdam, Vienna or Barcelona and in dozens of other cities and towns.

Usually during weekends, holidays and class breaks, I traveled by myself with my thirty-dollars-per-month Eurail Pass on the great European express trains throughout Europe and into North Africa. It was beyond belief that I could jump aboard any train without even having to make a reservation. I could sit anywhere in the first-class section of the train. This was such a far cry from my ride through the southern U.S. in a locked compartment and what was going on in 1961 in the U.S. with sit-ins and soon to come freedom rides.

Following World War II Europeans or other foreigners could not qualify for the Eurail Pass and had to make reservations for the train and pay the substantially higher regular fare. It was only for Americans. To get the Eurail Pass each month, all I had to do was go to the American Express office in Paris, prove I was an American by showing my U.S. passport and paying thirty dollars. Then I could enjoy a month of train rides through Europe. A black American could travel first class in Europe in 1961 without question.

Black Americans in the U.S. were forced to endure the most dehumanizing aspects of segregation, while black Americans like me traveled first class in Europe. This was the reality of 1961 and I was experiencing the two worlds. It was more than distressing to me to know that the reality was beyond my ability to affect any modicum of change in the U.S.

In Europe I felt a sense of humanity that I had never experienced in the U.S. before. In Europe I went to out of the ordinary parts of various countries and talked with strangers, and they reached out to me in a helpful and welcoming way. In the U.S. it was a rare occasion to have a similar personal encounter that I could experience.

I was enjoying in Europe the freeing of the chains being off of me. I was realizing that the U.S. was not representative of most of the rest of the world and certainly of Europe when it came to racism.

When I related my experiences on my train ride through the South twenty years earlier, to a friend who had been born and raised in segregated North Carolina he told me that I had seen more than he had personally seen because his family would not allow him to go into town or on public transportation throughout his life in North Carolina.

He later came to New York and after a doctoral degree became Superintendent of Schools in Bridgeport, Connecticut. I heard this reality many times from friends who lived in segregated Jim Crow South that they were not allowed to go into town. They were sheltered and amazed at my boldness because of the viciousness I could have experienced.

In Amsterdam on Fulbright

In Germany on Fulbright

One holiday week, I went to the southern tip of Spain, across the Straits of Gibraltar, and to North Africa, where I planned to venture further south through the Atlas Mountains to exotic Marrakesh in Morocco.

Winston E. Allen, Ph.D.

The Straits of Gibraltar crossing from Europe to Africa was rougher than usual and took longer than expected. When I arrived in Morocco the dock where we landed was pitch-black. After the departing passengers had been picked up by waiting cars and taxis, I was the sole person in the darkness and all facilities were closed for the night. I was approached by a Moroccan man in his twenties who asked me where I was going.

I told him I was on my way to Marrakesh by train, and he told me that the train station was closed for the night and that I could get my train in the morning. He then asked me in broken English, "Are you a Christian?"

I smartly answered, "No,"

He said, "What are you then?"

I told him that I was an agnostic.

That seemed to calm him down on the subject because he did not know any religion by that name.

I asked him his name, and he said, "Mohammed." He said, "I will show you where I live, and you can stay overnight at my place. In the morning I will show you how to get to the station for your train ride to Marrakesh." He was a lifesaver. I did not know what I would have done if it were not for Mohammed.

Marrakesh took me back centuries into another, exquisite world of camels, snake charmers and souks or outdoor markets packed with all kinds of copper ware, oriental rugs and handmade crafts. I was so delighted to be there and to be able to soak it all in. The people

40

were so friendly to me. I got to chat with many people and learn a bit about their lives.

They were curious about how and why I was there as I would have been, if I had been in their place. I was not a typical American tourist. I was a student on an extended trip to visit their world. I had to finally just try to keep it simple. I am just a curious guy who wanted to see how life was like in that part of Morocco and I'm happy to be here talking to you. They liked that and we had Moroccan tea together as we talked and they showed me around.

On another long weekend I went to Granada, Cordoba and Seville, in Spain featuring Moorish architecture. It was exquisite. I also went north to Stockholm, Sweden and to Oslo, Norway, up to the fiords and with its outdoor Vigeland sculpture museum.

One European City, Copenhagen, boasted of having a unique visitor's program, "Meet the Danes," in which Danish families hosted strangers who would be guests in their homes for a weekend. I arrived by train in Copenhagen, Denmark; simply picked up a green phone in the station; and spoke to a receptionist, who took down my name and gave me the name and address of a host family. I took a taxi to their home. Several families with whom I spent time with told me that having a black American as their weekend guest was a special treat because I was the first black person they had ever met. They all spoke English, and they peppered me with questions about my life in the U.S. They were eager to learn how difficult it was for a black man to live in the U.S. I told them some of my experiences.

It was a great way to meet perfect strangers and gain insight into their thinking, much of their life was different from our norms. I asked them about their country's socialist program: its free medical care, medical leave, and time off from work with pay for parents with newborn children. A few people I talked with seemed less than enthusiastic about what they were doing at work or where things were going for them.

They said that they had few anxieties about their standard of living and the security they were experiencing. The difference in income between different careers was not substantial so they could choose a career they were more passionate about and not one because it paid more money.

Attitudes about kids and sex seemed more permissive than in the States; they said that their teenage daughters, for example, were encouraged to have sleepovers with their boyfriends in their home. They said that it was better than having them hang out somewhere else.

On one occasion when I was walking in Copenhagen, a stranger walked up to me and said, "Sir, can I feel your hair?"

Although surprised I said, "Yes,"

She politely said, "Thank you."

That was the spirit of Copenhagen in 1961 when people were friendly.

I visited Copenhagen several times and each time I toured Tivoli Gardens with the hosts I was staying with, which was within walking distance of the amusement parks from their homes. Tivoli Gardens, opened in 1849 in the middle of the city, is one of the world's oldest-operating amusement parks. It actually served as a model for Disneyland in the U.S. It is a full year theme park with a lively mix of rides, attractions, gardens and restaurants that appeals to adults and children alike.

Each family I spent time with wanted to stroll through the park. In 1961, there were no lines and no tickets needed. Now there are tickets and long lines to get in, so the appeal of Tivoli Gardens continues. Strolling through the Tivoli Gardens and talking with my hosts gave me insights into the Danes' way of thinking, which was in many ways considerably different from the cultural norms I had grown accustomed to in the U.S.

In 1961, as a world history teacher, I sought out places that had particular historical appeal. One site stands out in my mind. I took a short trip from Paris to Amsterdam in the Netherlands to tour the secret annex where eleven-year-old Anne Frank and her family went into hiding from the Nazis. Anne Frank had been given a diary that she wrote in every day, detailing her experiences and feelings in the annex.

While sitting in an outside cafe in Paris one balmy afternoon, I heard a voice: "Hi, Win! What are you doing here?" It was Fran Cole, a niece of Nat King Cole. We were both shocked to see each other in Paris. After catching up, Fran told me that her fiancé, Al Fogelson, a Jewish guy she had met in New York, was arriving the next day and that it would be great if we could all meet for dinner the next evening there on the Champs-Élysées. After my classes at the Sorbonne and Fran's at the Paris Conservatory of Music, where she was studying piano, we all met for dinner.

I knew Fran Cole from my student days in New York. Fran had studied piano at the Juilliard School of Music, which was nearby. She was an accomplished concert pianist whom I saw in a performance later at Carnegie Hall.

Al told me that he had just gotten his annual bonus, and it came to a quarter of a million dollars, which was at that time the norm on Wall Street for traders who had had a good trading year. Al revealed to me how he had gone into the business after undergraduate school with no experience by walking into Goldman Sachs, a leading investment company, and signing up for the next trainee course with the commitment that he would get a trading position once he passed the entry examination. This caused me to see the stock market as a path for blacks to make real money, because getting and holding a job was not a path to wealth-building. I knew a host of blacks who were college graduates who had the skills and knowledge to pass the Series 7 examination but who worked in dead-end jobs.

I put my dreaming cap on and began to ponder, what if I were to become the catalyst and form my own company, bringing minority people and their associates to Wall Street? It seemed to me that Wall Street was at the heart of what made the U.S. financially dynamic. As a student of Economics, I needed to put my theories into practice and first find a Wall Street door that I could enter. I could not wait to get back to New York to see what I could do.

PART II
Wall Street 1962-1968

Chapter 6

Opening Wall Street in 1962

I returned from Paris in 1961 with a determination to become a trainee at one of the traditional firms and overcome any expected barriers. First, I approached Goldman Sachs by telephone, and I was told after they reviewed my résumé that I sent to them and to come in the next week to start classes. Little did I know, they were thinking I was a white person because I am told I speak without a black dialect. Whatever the reason, I had no trouble getting appointments over the phone. Can you imagine the look on their faces when I walked through the door and told them who I was and that I was ready for class? They were shocked!

After I told them who I was, I heard one of them say to a colleague "This colored guy wants me to put him into this class that's starting today." She then came back and said to me "sorry the class is full." Each time that I phoned ahead I got the okay to come in for the trainee course. When I arrived I received the same story. I was able to get registered over the phone, but then the door was slammed shut. "The training course that you applied for is filled up." I was told the same story each time. I realized how Al Fogelson a white guy, with no experience, received red carpet treatment from Goldman Sachs, while I with stellar credentials couldn't get in the front door.

Investment firms like any other corporation, could choose who they wanted in their company, so there was nothing I could do. However, there must be another route for me and I needed to find it quickly.

Why work for someone who is unable to recognize your value. I knew that I was uniquely qualified for a position.

I learned through some research that there was one other method of entry that the large firms took. They became independent broker-dealers. I wanted to see how I could gain entry that way. Although I had stellar credentials, I knew that it was going to be very tough to become an independent anything in Wall Street, but I refused to be deterred. I read up on being an independent broker-dealer and I made an immediate appointment by phone to meet with an official at the Securities and Exchange Commission (SEC). After setting up a meeting on the phone to go in and start on the path to a broker-dealership, I entered at the appointed time.

You have no idea the look on their faces when I walked into the SEC and said after talking to you on the phone that I was Winston Allen, here to pursue the path to becoming an independent broker-dealer. I was immediately told that there must be some mistake. The head person at the time was called in. He said to me, "I apologize that you were misled. You have come to the wrong place. We at the SEC do not deal with broker-dealers."

To overcome this barrier because it was contrary to what I had read, I rushed over to the New York City Public Library nearby at Fortieth Street and Fifth Avenue to seek a conclusive answer to my question about becoming an independent broker-dealer. I had just received from the SEC The Securities Exchange Act of 1934 states, "Brokers and Dealers must register with the SEC and join a self-regulatory organization, namely the National Association of Securities Dealers (NASD), to do investment business, now known as FINRA (Financial Industry Regulatory Authority)."

Being turned around by the SEC attendants slowed me down a bit, but this hurdle did not deter me from my goal. By this time, I had the evidence that there were four requirements to becoming an independent broker-dealer: (1) be a college graduate, (2) pass a background check, (3) pass all applicable NASD exams, and (4) provide a minimum net capital amount. When I went back to the SEC for a follow-up visit, the next person I saw told me, "Consider looking elsewhere for a more suitable venture. Broker-dealer firms do not start with a single individual."

The SEC official then said, "To run the business of an independent broker-dealer firm requires a sizable endowment with a large reserve capital, a staff of accountants, attorneys and compliance officers. In addition, the firm has to maintain a sizable 'net capital' for the duration of the firm's existence and be sufficiently capitalized and staffed to manage random audits and fines for any violations, with sizable penalties."

I realized that I had discovered a not-widely-known way in which I could become a licensed broker-dealer and market stocks and bonds directly through my own business. I did not believe that the barriers and hurdles that they were detailing could not be overcome by me, so I asked for an NASD manual. The attendant left the room to check. When she returned, she said, "We are all out of NASD manuals."

I repeatedly telephoned the SEC. Finally, I got an attendant who said we have manuals. I went immediately and got the manual. I read and re-read through all nine thousand pages. There were rules and procedures I had to know thoroughly to do business as an independent broker-dealer. I submerged myself in the voluminous rules and regulations of the industry.

I needed to go through the NASD screening: interviews questionnaires, and exam questions. I worked at it for many months. The nine thousand fourteen pages included corporate organization, rules of the National Association of Securities Dealers (NASD) association, business conduct, marketplace rules and procedural rules.

My goal was to complete the entire process by the end of the year. The data showed me that the stock market business was poised to take advantage of a surge in American industrial earnings over the next few years. That was my motivation. I was in the process of completing the requirements and met the net capital rule by meeting the required net capital amount which I placed in an investment company account as required, where it would stay for the duration of my company.

After completing the process, overcoming the barriers, hurdles and obstacles, there was nothing for them to do but license me. I became licensed by the NASD. I became a general securities principal of my broker-dealer firm and on December 2, 1962, I received an acceptance letter from the NASD. The news was especially gratifying because the long struggle that I had experienced was over. I had become the first black owner and founder of an independent broker-dealer firm in the U.S.

I now had a Wall Street independent broker-dealership with all the rights and privileges of any securities firm. I opened my firm in Manhattan and became my own boss. That was fulfilling to me as I had achieved my goals at a perilous time in the U.S. during the era of the Civil Rights Movement. I would be able to help narrow the unequitable distribution of wealth in the U.S. by clearing a path for overlooked people on Wall Street that had previously been excluded.

National Association of Securities Dealers, Inc.

District No. 12 Committee

JOHN W. CALLAGHAN, Chairman, New York   GEORGE T. FLYNN, Vice Chairman, New York

ELLIOTT ALLEN	NEW YORK		H. STANLEY KRUGEN	NEW YORK
ALLAN C. CUSTIS, JR.	NEW YORK		DANIEL V. McNAMEE	ALBANY
H. THEODORE ANKELAND	NEW YORK		VICTOR M. MILLER	NEW YORK
ROBERT H. GARDNER	NEW YORK		JONAS K. OTTENS	NEW YORK
HERBERT A. GOLDSTONE	NEW YORK		ALFRED J. ROSS	NEW YORK
WARREN C. KEIDEL	HARTFORD		WARREN K. VAN HISE	NEWARK
JAMES F. KEARNEY	NEW YORK		JOHN WASSERMAN	NEW YORK
JOSEPH D. KRAKOWICH	NEW YORK		CLEVELAND E. WHITE	NEW YORK

GEORGE J. BERGEN, Secretary
25 BROAD STREET
NEW YORK 4, N. Y.
DIGBY 4-7680

December 3, 1962

Mr. Winston E. Allen
5550 Fieldston Road
Bronx 71, New York

Dear Mr. Allen:

We are pleased to learn that you have been admitted to membership in this Association. Your listing places you in District No. 12 which comprises the States of New York, Connecticut and northern New Jersey.

When you were admitted to membership, you agreed to abide by the rules of our Association. Since those rules codify the principles upon which our members operate and establish standards to which they are held accountable, we urge you to read them carefully so that you may be thoroughly familiar with them.

To assist you to remain in compliance with our rules, we have attached hereto an "Operational Check List" which we trust you will study frequently enough to assure yourself that you are consistently operating your firm in accordance with the rules and policies of the Board of Governors of the Association which are presently in effect.

As a new member, the significance and importance of some of the points covered in the Check List may not be immediately evident. Since your success and well being in the industry is dependent on your meeting established standards, it is suggested that if you have questions concerning the Association's Rules, you arrange an appointment with a member of this staff for the purpose of securing an explanation.

Very truly yours,

George J. Bergen
Secretary, District No. 12

Enclosure

Chapter 7

Prospects

The founding of my firm in 1962 occurred shortly before the biggest surge in mutual fund history. The Wall Street mutual fund surge had begun. There was about $4 billion in mutual funds throughout the U.S. in 1963, and within five years, that figure more than tripled, passing $13 billion by the end of 1968. Everything that happened in the sixties was a mere opening act for the seventies. At the start of the boom, the mood of the investment business was exuberant.

Everyone, it seemed, was convinced that the benefits of capitalism were at least being expanded, although not to ordinary folks. The prevailing view was still that Wall Street was for the rich. The most compelling claim against capitalism was that the ownership of industrial wealth was going to be concentrated in the hands of the very few and that we were doomed to failure. Who could deny that the spreading to blacks of ownership, the goal toward which my firm strove, would be a rewarding task and accomplishment for American society?

For me the American dream was by no means simply the acquisition and ownership of resources and property. It meant financial independence. It also would allow me to determine for myself how best to spend my time, and it allowed the doors of creativity, philanthropy and other fulfilling endeavors to be opened to me. My vision included becoming self-fulfilled and able to do what I was most passionate about. As an entrepreneur, I would be able to organize a business and hire people dedicated to opening one of the U.S.'s paths to wealth-building.

Although harrowing to become licensed, the business was showing that it was a fast track to wealth-building once I could build a client base for my sales. I was now on my own and needed to find the investment path, products and prospects.

Traditionally, investment industry firms have taken their names from founders and owners, for example, Goldman Sachs, Lehman Brothers, J.P. Morgan. In the 1960s, my decision was to adopt the name which represented a departure from that tradition and highlighted our mission, one not found elsewhere in the industry in 1962. Our mission statement had been designed to illustrate what sets us apart. Creative Investor Services (Creative) was the first broker-dealer firm in the U.S. with black ownership. It was charting a new path. It represented something created rather than something inherited or imitated.

Two years after I started my company, I began conducting public seminars to give newcomers to Wall Street the fundamentals and basics of investing. In short, I provided customers with the best of both worlds: an expansion of the knowledge base and personal attention to individual investment needs. Creative developed a reputation for having introduced some new and profitable investment vehicles for new investors available at that time. Demonstrating the ways in which a second income could be developed for individuals who placed their hard-earned discretionary dollars into selected mutual funds, I thereby built a community of investors who have remained loyal clients for decades.

Creative found that the previous denial of the profit potential to black people of modest means only exacerbated the income and wealth disparity that had grown steadily in the United States. Creative has been proud to help its clients pursue their financial goals while giving them more time to focus on what really matters, building wealth and income. Shares in a fund could be invested in many industries, and if, as usually is the case, many smart investors saw a rise in value in the shares of their funds, then their assets gave them increased leverage.

Many saw their invested value in open-end mutual funds doubling in net asset value in less than eight years. Investors were sold on the investments. The funds that were invested in were redeemable immediately by a customer for any reason. Because of this, the advantages of investing in an open-end mutual fund were combined with the blessing of the greatest feature of such a fund, liquidity. With history reinforcing the natural advantages of liquidity, the mutual fund concept made astonishing inroads upon the new wealth.

The mechanism of open-end mutual funds, with emphasis on liquidity, meant that my investors could cash out at any time and get their net asset value in cash. This abolished some of the fears of investing held by the black community. It was entirely possible in the early sixties to regard the mutual fund as a promising tool for economic justice. I perceived that the open-end investment vehicle was the instrument I would use to resolve the cruel conflict that kept black investors of modest means out of the investment market. This was of great import to reduce substantially the risks of investing for the small investor, because if such risks were not mitigated, the investor could very easily have lost money when the market was going down.

Still there was the period from 1951 to 1961, a span of time in which the market went up by 175 percent. Anyone taking out a new program in 1962, the year I launched Creative, was ideally placed to realize a substantial gain if he simply sat on his investment for a ten-year period. Creative's idealized portrait of the smart mutual fund investment mechanism seemed totally in sync with the needs of its constituents. In the postwar world, Creative was moving swiftly with the wind at its back.

Chapter 8
My Selling Securities, 1963

I soon realized that selling had become a passion of mine and that I enjoyed the one-on-one interactions with my clients. I immediately began selling a few high-performing mutual funds to the people I knew and their friends in New York City and Westchester, N.Y., a bedroom community in the suburbs of N.Y. My first two selections of funds were the Oppenheimer Fund and Fidelity Funds. I made it a point to approach and get to know the officers of the funds that I promoted. Don Spiro, president of Oppenheimer Fund came to my office in Manhattan when I became a prime seller of his fund.

I built a community of interested investors who had never thought of owning stocks as an investment. My clients were motivated by their dream of financial security, college education for their children and money for retirement. They were middle-income families, frequently with two breadwinners, whom I helped to realize that to achieve their goals, they needed to have their discretionary funds invested each month and working for them. I persuaded, educated and encouraged them to invest their hard-earned money in diverse fields of high performing securities.

Many of the securities suggested to my clients were systematic long-term investment programs that minimized the risk of loss of capital from the inevitable downturns in the stock market. My clients were willing and able to proceed with investment programs and had confidence that Creative would be there to service their investments and handle their inquiries. I believed I was singularly the most equipped person to tackle this market and show how my investors could benefit from the market's growth at that time.

I had an international economics background and a personal connection with the people I was approaching. No other firm or individual that I knew was similarly involved with the black community, so my competition was almost nonexistent. After a while, prospects sought me out to help them invest their discretionary funds into the securities market. I knew my client base personally and their ability and desire to capitalize on the opportunities that were out there. I knew how to motivate them to pursue their goals. I had face-to-face contact with my prospects. That was natural for me. It helped me make marketing presentations to broaden my client base.

I enjoyed working with people, and they enjoyed working with me. When I first began I was an independent NASD broker-dealer as my primary occupation and a high school teacher as well. At the time, I did not know how long I would be able to do both interests to my satisfaction. Two primary risks for Creative were that the investment of time and money would take some time to build a solid profit base and my interest in expanding my teaching career would suffer a loss.

To my gratification, my client base grew rapidly. I went from a handful of prospects to over a hundred in a very short time. Client interaction was necessary but time consuming. Approaching marketing from the customer's perspective, I asked my clients what in their lives they wanted to see changed, something that additional funds could affect. By visiting the homes of prospective clients and learning about their situations firsthand, and their aspirations for their children and themselves, I was inspired to continue my pursuit.

I continued to acquire the necessary knowledge regarding selected high performing stocks, bonds and mutual funds and how to create wealth for my clients. Some of my middle-aged clients had heard stories of the great stock market crash of 1929 and the ensuing Great Depression, but they were also aware of fortunes being made by those who owned shares in the stock market. They had to be assured that they could do much better through carefully selected, high-performing investments, that could greatly outperform their more familiar traditional bank accounts.

The time commitment and the success that I was experiencing were too much for me to handle alone. I would not be able to continue as a one-man operation for long as the increase in the number of my clients would not allow me the time to continue to service the growing number of prospects. Word of mouth was generating customers, but I wanted to fully exploit my independent broker-dealership and bring newly licensed people into the field of investing. I decided, that since established reps were not likely to come with a new fledging firm, to seek out new reps.

Chapter 9
My Crash Course Created Salesmen, 1964–1967

To fulfill a pledge to my client base for the highest development and standards that this full-service investment firm would produce, Creative needed to build a fast-growing trained staff. It was a major challenge because there was not a reservoir of licensed representatives for me to draw from. I quickly decided to recruit and train my own professionals and I immediately began a drive to find, train and recruit, prospects for my company's growth. This lack of recruits was another opportunity to use rejections to my advantage.

I set my goal at having sixty registered reps as part of Creative within a three-year period. Finding people who were committed to my blueprint and equipping them to be productive was a hurdle that I had to overcome. The prospect for success was not great, and the feedback I received from contemporaries in the business world showed doubt that it could be done. Despite this obstacle, I reassured myself that this was the right move for my business at that time and that I would be successful.

The first gate of entry to investments for an investment representative was the NASD Series 7 exam. The primary aim of each prospect was to pass the very difficult National Association of Securities Dealers NASD Series 7 exam to become licensed as a registered rep with the NASD and with my firm. If you did not pass that exam you're out. I immediately began to place prospects wanted ads in newspapers that were targeted to a minority readership. The ads for motivated prospects brought in dozens of responses, each time and from those I was able to glean twenty-four prospects. I could not handle all the applicants at once, so I had to stagger them. That was the beginning of the growth of Creative.

Because all our prospective reps were new to the field, I had to structure a very technical course that was designed for a novice to understand. My prospects were unfamiliar with Wall Street language, so I developed unique modules for what I called my crash course. I met the prospects in small groups, and after an introductory session, I determined who would come back for my one-month NASD crash course. There was no more natural a question for the prospects to ask me than "Is it very difficult to pass this exam?" Later I was able to say, "Dozens have already passed."

This meant for trainees a commitment to a one-month series of classes and mountains of homework. Those who would become registered reps with Creative knew that they would earn sizable commissions for the investment products they sold.

At six in the evening on the third Monday of every month, a dozen or more hopefuls would assemble in my office to start their crash course. I had the job of teaching them to pass the grueling exam. They had mountains of homework and each schedule had pre-exam tests. Before taking the Series 7 exam, each applicant took my pre-exam test. After passing my exam, they were scheduled for the NASD exam. Results were astounding. Upon passing the NASD Series 7 pre-exam, they all received well-earned accommodations. Fifty passed the exam the first time.

My one-month crash course to pass the NASD Series 7 examination allowed me to staff up quickly. Every one of these applicants became licensed registered reps with my firm, Creative. Once the exam was passed, I then conducted sales training sessions in which I explained the realities of a sales career with my sales reps. I explained to them that they were entering a field in which they could be a critical factor in the lives of many people. However, I made it clear that this was hard work and they would be compensated on their performance.

Chapter 10

Marketing Smart Investments, 1964–1968

After passing the Series 7 exam, my trainees took a second crash course. In my second crash course, I directed the trainees to determine their prospects' investment objectives, education, future income and retirement needs. I also coached trainees on how to preplan a presentation, properly meet a prospect, use the telephone effectively and handle objections. Modules that I developed for the sales training marketing sessions on selling investments were designed to meet the clients' need for more income and increased security and ultimately morph into something even more important: the ability to take control of their financial lives.

I structured role-playing practice exercises to simulate sales interactions with a client and make the transition to selling securities easier. Through role-playing, my sales reps could see themselves through a new lens, correct their errors and gain confidence. In addition, I added modules that taught my sales reps how to prospect and how to qualify any prospective customer by making certain that he or she had the necessary discretionary funds to invest.

I discussed with them a step-by-step approach to achieve their and their client's objectives. With this formula for success, my sales reps were able to develop positive attitudes, focus on the development of their sales skills and set out to earn their commissions. As my firm grew, they prospered.

I concluded my sales training course by teaching my sales reps at the close what I learned to do early in my career. After the closing question, shut up! In other words, whenever you ask a closing question, stop talking! The first person to speak loses. This is much more difficult to do than it sounds, and it takes practice. I encouraged each of my sales reps to remember this when they made an offer to a customer.

I had to motivate the reps to want to sell. I asked many rhetorical questions, for example, "Do you want to be used by the capitalist system, or do you want to use it?" It was catechism, in which the right answers seemed obvious. The most important question was stated implicitly and explicitly in the title of my first book, *Don't Get Mad, Get Rich: Become Financially Independent.*

Each salesman began his career by walking into my office and trying to sell me his investment package. After each exercise, I would meet with the rep, and we would sit down together and go through the strengths and weaknesses in their presentation.

I titled my crash course Marketing Smart Investments. There were lengthy group sessions where I and my reps picked over the techniques of their presentations. They practiced firm handshakes and sincere smiles in front of mirrors. I impressed upon them that they should always try to sit next to a prospect, rather than across the table from him or her. That way it is easier to win the prospect's support.

In my first book, *Don't Get Mad, Get Rich,* I have a chapter on the theory and methodology of goals. Do you want to put forth the effort to be rich? This is a question I asked my trainees. For most people, the answer was yes. They would say they would like to be rich, or would not mind becoming rich, but they sincerely wanted an easy way. My question was calculated to sort out the attitudes of my reps. For those who said yes, they did sincerely want to be rich; there was a logical follow-through. If that was what they really wanted, they must do what they needed to do, and then I would try to help them become rich.

The sales training course bore the aspect of a sales pitch to the reps. I would explain to them that after one month's sales training, they would have to be able to go out and sell mutual funds to complete strangers. I would explain that they had to master one fundamental secret: always control the conversation with the prospect. The basic tool that the Creative reps were first equipped with was a test case in the form of a dialogue between sales rep and prospect, which the sales rep was expected to learn by heart. Delivery time was no more than fifteen minutes.

It is a vital principle that a rep needs to anticipate every objection a prospect might make. But if a prospect were to break through and raise an objection that had not been anticipated, the question should first be restated. Even now, sales reps of my training class who rose to be executives tell me that they fall back on the sales techniques they learned in my crash course, adding that they know their success grew in direct proportion to what they had learned and their competence. Sales reps, for instance, especially dreaded cold calls, which they had to do when they ran out of prospects and had to contact a prospect unannounced. We prepared by developing techniques on how to handle this type of situation.

Salespeople of any sort are creatures of motivation and ambition. They are likely to be approached as a target to join another firm now that they were producing, especially if those offers come baited with an additional percentage of income. The team that I assembled was a particularly stable one. To insulate such reps for a decade against most of the wiles was a considerable feat of business, and I overcame the competition and got it done.

A good many of those who had sincerely wanted to be rich achieved their purpose. They may not have become as rich as they wanted or thought they should be, but they had developed skills and a sense of accomplishment that they could always use and rely upon.

There are a number of reasons why my reps found satisfaction. What some of my sales reps said is that this was one of the few opportunities where they could be themselves and in essence do what they wanted to do. This is noticeable in the photographs within these pages, taken at various Creative's seminars, where leadership was exhibited and reps were able to directly interact with the public, both individually and collectively.

Reps also appreciated the fact that they had the freedom to become as successful as they could become as there was no income ceiling. They could go into each day with a daily challenge. In most other businesses they had been in, they had no challenge to look forward to because income was fixed. But a sales rep could go from the heights of exhilaration to the depths of discouragement within two days, then climb back to the heights of exhilaration the next day.

Many of the reps said that before joining Creative, they had been doing something that was not satisfying. They said that it was a particular thrill to know they had helped someone when they went home and said, "I got another family happily involved in what the systematic investment program will do for them and how it will change their life." Many said that the better their skills, the better they were at sales, and the greater benefit they could give to their clients and their clients' families, who otherwise would not have been able to reach their goals.

The reps took the position that no one limited their growth but themselves. They felt that if they worked harder, they would be paid for their extra effort with extra results. Most reps said that they had had jobs and even professions that could not fulfill their potential as they knew it to be. I started with many who had just put their foot on the lowest rung of the ladder before joining Creative, and many of them climbed high on their ladder of potential because they were firm believers that there is nothing to the myth of the natural-born sales wonder. It took hard work.

There were three grades in our sales force, which depended upon the volume of sales made: each registered rep started as a basic salesperson, then rose to advanced salesperson and then reaching the level of career senior. With each promotion, the salesperson received a larger share of the sales charge extracted from the transaction upon each sale. Above these three ranks were three more: supervisor, group manager and branch manager. In order to break into these upper levels, it was necessary to actually recruit other salespeople. Promotion through these ranks depended partly upon further recruitment, partly upon the volume of sales made by the superior or manager and his or her team.

The new expansion of mutual fund growth capitalized on two propositions. One was that there was a new addition of black people available to become investors and armed with a prospectus and other data to help in translating financial terms into language that ordinary people could understand. The second was that such people, exactly like wealthier investors, were eager to make money with their money.

Previously, the manager of mutual funds had tended to assume that it was his or her job to employ the client's money to buy a mixture of good class shares and bonds, and leave it there, regardless of peaks and valleys in the graph of stock exchange prices. The new view was that the investors wanted a mutual fund manager to be constantly looking for new growth shares and to move their money into those shares.

My reps did not merely copy a pitch and remain content with it. My reps ceaselessly polished and remodeled the presentation my salespeople used. From time to time, however, stock markets actually do fall. Suppose selected stocks are going down and the market derails. Selected stocks must still be worth buying, but not for the same amount of money. You can buy even more of them and get better value for your money that way. The flaw, of course, is that some shares may fall and never rise again, but hopefully not the stocks you have selected.

Chapter 11

Becoming a Successful Manager in My Firm, 1964–1970

Why is it that the rich may invest in the wealth created by capitalism and thereby increase their assets? It is because the poor have few dollars left over from purchasing the necessities of life. They cannot afford to tie up anything in investments, so the working class become their subjects.

Through the Creative salespeople, the people they contact are enabled to turn their investment fund savings into shares in a fund. Skilled people invest their surplus funds in shares of many industrial concerns. If, as should normally be the case, most of these are positive.

Over the long term investments rise in value, then the rise increases the value of each share of the fund. Consequently, the savings multiply, and the fund ensures that it will always redeem a customer's shares immediately, for cash. Thus, the advantages of investment are combined with the blessings of investment's great opposite, liquidity. Capitalism was able to be employed to bring about that equitable distribution of wealth, which is the aim of socialism. This idealized portrait of the open-end fund is consistent with reality.

The objective was that everyone willing to work and save could participate in their own wealth-building development through my firm. That was my dream for beginning to minimize the huge wealth disparity in the U.S. within the structure of the free enterprise system.

I was convinced that what was good for the American investor, whom I was approaching, was good for the U.S. economy.

My further conviction was that capitalism had a rightful place in the lives of blacks and all Americans. To me it was not what you had; it was what you did financially with what you had. My timing could not have been better, because over the next decade, the 1960's, I was set to expand the number of blacks now included in open-end investment companies and Creative was set to alter the financial landscape of the U.S.

I had to encourage self-starting individuals whom I met, to think big about moving beyond solely being an employee and a consumer. What I suggested to them also entailed their focusing on owning and controlling a share in the U.S. I often knew that what those who had the potential to move beyond the limitations of a single source of income needed was to develop the habit of thinking big. If all they thought about was getting and holding a job, they probably would never get on the path to building wealth, since they would avoid any conditioning to think on a big scale.

I would encourage them not to get on a salary treadmill, as a final step. As a businessman, I had to possess certain character traits that I prided myself on: being assertive, bold and courageous and having optimism and a willingness to take controlled risks. To be a successful businessman, I had to be sure of myself. This helped me to be able to handle all types of personalities. It was important that I centered my business on something that my reps really wanted to do and were gifted at. I sometimes worked at it for sixty to eighty hours or more a week, so I needed to be excited about getting to work to ensure success.

To me, to be an effective leader was similar to being an orchestra conductor, that is, to be able to work with people with differing skills yet be able to get those individuals to become successful and achieve the goals I set for my company and hopefully the goals that they set for themselves. I recognized that my primary role as a leader was to take on the function of clearing the path toward the objectives of the business.

I prided myself on having a group of diverse and talented people with strong personalities who worked together toward a common goal. I had to have problem-solving skills, inventiveness and the ability to delegate authority. Most importantly, I had to be able to make plans with long-term goals and have a capacity for hard work to overcome any hurdles. We were not exclusive to any group and our client was racially diverse. We had two productive non-minority reps.

It was always intriguing to observe the variety of backgrounds of the Creative staff and clients, the differences in personalities and the range of their interests. The goal that I had set in Creative was to ensure that the reps had an environment where they could become as proficient as possible. I tried to give them every opportunity to project themselves and realize their full potential. During the Creative seminars, for example, reps and managers played a major role in planning, organizing and interacting with the attendees at the events.

Being an entrepreneur is not for everyone. For many people, the American dream is to have a great job, not to have one's own business. Many people are content to acclimate to the environment they're in rather than control it. Entrepreneurs, however, want to take control of their destinies rather than being controlled by them.

I needed to be optimistic and see opportunities where others saw problems. The most important preparation I had for success was to acquire knowledge of the business and the marketplace. To be successful, I had to be able to identify what consumers needed and what they wanted to buy. Sometimes I recognized a consumer's need and launched a marketing campaign before consumers even saw that need.

Chapter 12
Wealth-Building Seminars, 1965–1967

Creative sponsored Wall Street wealth-building seminars, held semiannually at the Americana Hotel near Lincoln Center in Manhattan. It always drew a full house from 1965 through 1967. They were inspirational seminars. Attendees said that they learned more about the handling of money and the investment process in these meetings than they had ever learned before. As an illustration, the rule of 72 shows how long it will take for your investment to double in value, based on the rate of return.

Most of the attendees viewing the announcement that I had placed in local newspapers would probably have glossed over it, believing that the ad was not seriously meant for them. But through word of mouth and people-to-people contact, many people had come to conclude that this was the type of seminar for them. It was a complimentary seminar with an attached raffle ticket for a stock prize. The raffle prize was an open-end mutual funds. Hundreds of reps would meet with attendees at their homes to invite their participation in Creative's wealth-building program.

CEO Winston Allen Opening Seminar in 1964

Winston E. Allen, Ph.D.

Master of Ceremonies

Master of Ceremonies

74

Creative Investor Services seminar with Oppenheimer Management Corporation presenter sitting to the left of Winston.

Winston E. Allen, Ph.D.

Audience Participation

The Speaker explains the "rule of 72"

Seminar Audience

Winston E. Allen, Ph.D.

The Speaker answers questions

Questions addressed to the Speaker

Winston E. Allen, Ph.D.

A Second Presenter

Attendees at Creative's Seminar

Selecting A Raffle Contest Winner

President Greets Winner

President gives 30 shares of mutual fund stock to winner

Conferring on future plans

Winston E. Allen, Ph.D.

Second winner receives 10 shares of mutual fund stock

Attendee Congratulates President

Creative's Affiliates

Social Hour after our Seminar

Winston E. Allen, Ph.D.

Discussing investing issues

Winston and Matt

Matt Snell and Mrs Snell

Meet and Greet

Managers of Creative Investor Services

My firm developed its client base against the backdrop of sit-ins and the Freedom Rides, which were broadcast worldwide. The media at the time, drew us to the struggle for civil rights, which our membership was involved with. Each seminar produced clients. Passing out leaflets, setting up programs, and enlisting instructors all culminated in attracting vehemently interested and energized participants. I had shown that my heart was sound by paying for all the seminar costs out of my own pocket. There seemed to be a moment just before the climax of every great solicited event when even the sturdiest skeptics said to themselves. This is for real.

With a salesman's flair for divining what an audience wants and needs to hear, I delivered my closing remarks with two themes. The first detailed the glories of the market and the confidence in the potential of Wall Street for wealth-building. As I concluded, I said, "We all need to get aboard." I then turned to my second theme, my own company. I predicted that by 1968 this company would have trained and placed in the field eighty reps with $10 million worth of client investments.

Chapter 13

The New York Times Highlighted My Successful Firm, July 31, 1968

The New York Times story of my firm broke through the alarming news of the assassination of Martin Luther King Jr. on April 4, 1968, Robert Kennedy's murder on June 6, 1968, anti–Vietnam War riots and occupation of Columbia University and other universities by students in the spring of 1968, and the impending largest teacher strike for community control of schools in New York's history set for September of that same year.

When the story of the overwhelming success with my crash course appeared in the Financial and Business section on July 31, 1968, captioned "Crash Course Creates Salesmen," it rocked the marketplace nationwide. After *The New York Times* highlighted the successes, large Wall Street brokerage firms suddenly saw the possibilities for a new market including Goldman Sachs. I realized that I could achieve my goals of bringing this wealth-building to the minority community in a shorter time span than I had expected.

The increased awareness was quite evident through the coverage on television and the feedback that we were receiving from viewers. This affected me as it pulled our company into the front pages of many newspapers and other media around the country. Black working community members saw that they were now taken seriously as investors.

It was evident that there was a compelling need for this type of article in July 1968 and they rushed it into print after researching and after immediately meeting with me for a few hours. The press wrote articles about how this company had broken the Wall Street barriers, in the face of overcoming the hurdles.

Also, the media were curious as to how a hundred Creative reps were able to set spectacular records involving novice investors who had come to accept the financial-planning strategies set up by Creative and had found clients who were willing and able to invest their hard-earned money into individually selected investments with programs selected for clients based on their particular profiles. Creative and its reps received acclaim and admiration from the media and the financial community when the story broke.

Gaining national publicity in *The New York Times* was the big opportunity about my company with my photograph that appeared on the front of the business section on July 31, 1968. It was a masterstroke of publicity. Although it was unsolicited and its timing was unexpected, the article caused a rush of activity when it hit the newsstand.

In 1968 how did my business methods come to be covered on the front page of the business section of the *Times*? About a week earlier while attending a cocktail party at one of my neighbor's homes in Larchmont, I was speaking to the host Hal Levine and he asked me what I was presently doing? I told him about the company that I had founded that was making a mark in the world of finance by training a cadre of people who were in dead-end jobs to enter the citadel of capitalism, Wall Street. As the evening moved on, I knew I had piqued his interest, as we talked more about my company. He seemed quite interested that I was CEO in a pioneer venture in the world of finance.

He continued with more questions. I told him that my clients were inner-city folks who were interested in finance and I was developing a new and sizable market. We talked about how I had built my company from scratch by recruiting and training new salesmen to take the NASD licensing exam and then training them to sell securities. Before we parted that evening, he asked me to call the following Monday morning at his office at the Pan Am Building in Manhattan. We exchanged business cards. I then realized I was talking to Hal Levine, President of his Public Relations firm.

On Monday morning when I called him, his secretary put me right through to him. He told me that he had someone who wanted to meet me and that I should come to his office at noon the following day, Tuesday. I cleared my calendar and went down to see him. When I got to his office, he told me that Robert D. Hershey, Jr., a Finanial Correspondent for *The New York Times Business Section*, was waiting for me at the Algonquin Hotel nearby and he gave me the address.

Hershey and I had long conversations in which he asked questions about Creative, my recruitment efforts, my activities in expanding the sales force of my investment firm, and about me personally. I talked about the problems that I first had in recruiting registered reps that forced me to create a training program as a way to staff the company. Building the broker-dealer business the old-fashioned way, from the bottom up, caught the executive's interest. We talked for hours about what I had been doing with my company. I sensed that the newspapers, always looking for novel and interesting stories, would be very interested in Creative.

Hershey wanted photographs to go with the story, so we went to the Times office to take the photos. When we finished, I explained to Hershey how busy I was at the time, with classes and commitments piling up and my business commitments. I felt I couldn't handle any publicity coming at this time. He assured me that there would be no story without my first knowing about it and promised to call me before the story went to press. It was about 4:30 when we parted.

I had been taking a summer doctoral course in statistics with Professor John Waldron at the Fordham University Graduate School so that I could complete my preliminary coursework early and get a jump on the other matriculation requirements. About 9:00 AM the next morning, Wednesday, July 31, 1968, Professor Waldron entered our classroom and said that he had an announcement to make before class began. He smiled slowly and said, "Class I think we need to take a moment to acknowledge a celebrity in our midst." He dramatically pulled out *The New York Times*. Although there had been no call from Hershey, the story was on the newsstand. Professor Waldron separated the business section from the rest of the paper and held it up to the class. On the front page, above the fold, was a large picture of me. I was astounded. The class applauded.

Crash Course Creates Salesmen. This one single article had the most profound effect on me and my business and sparked a tidal wave of media coverage and public appearances. The story covered my successful effort in recruiting and training new registered reps for my growing investment firm. That one story changed my life and my career for the next thirty-five years. This publicity was an acknowledgment and an endorsement of my company and its development. This story was featured by *Orlando Florida Star*, the *Chicago Tribune*, the *Richmond Times Dispatch* and the *Cincinnati Enquirer*, as well as television and radio appearances, including *WOR Stock Market Observer.*

Many television program appearances and business presentations followed the publications of the story in *The New York Times* with *Westchester Business Journal* and *Finance Magazine* interviews. It was evident that there was a compelling need for this type of article in July 1968 and they rushed it into print after researching and after immediately meeting with me for a few hours. The press wrote articles about how this company had broken the Wall Street barriers, in the face of hurdles.

Also, the media were curious as to how a hundred Creative reps were able to set spectacular records involving novice investors who had come to accept the financial-planning strategies set up by Creative and had found clients who were willing and able to invest their hard-earned money into individually selected investments with programs selected for clients based on their particular profiles. Creative and its reps received acclaim and admiration from the media and the financial community when the stories broke. This was evidenced by Don Spiro, president of Oppenheimer Funds, who sent his acclamation complimenting us on our record.

Almost as gratifying as the *Time's* article and the media attention that followed were the numerous letters that followed from perfect strangers who were delighted in what I had been able to accomplish. The letters came from those who wanted to know how they could become a part of the organization and those who had an interest in Wall Street and in selling. Many were interested in taking my crash course or joining the company. They cited their interest in sales, hunger for new careers, and some dissatisfaction with their job or their accomplishments. The letters, calls and articles flowed continuously after that and it was clear that Creative was the right fit for those who were seeking additional careers and interested in financial planning services.

Most of the coverage I received was about someone who put his theories into practice. The media was also quick to pick up the fact that I dispelled the myth that business could not be conducted in the black community. What began as an untapped market for my company soon became a nationally known story about the leading black-owned broker-dealer firm in the country. I also made note in interviews that while I might be doing something spectacular, credit also had to be given to others, like my team of registered reps and the community of investors that we were servicing. We also realized that we were realizing our goal of bringing wealth-building to the minority community in a shorter time span than was planned.

New York Times, "Crash Course Creates Salesmen." Feature story about
Winston Allen and his company, Creative Investor Services, 1968.

FINANCE

DECEMBER 1969
VOL. 87   NO. 12

Winston Allen featured in Finance Magazine

PART III

Director, Corporate Executive and Entrepeneur

Chapter 14

Directing The College Discovery Program and Fordham University, 1968–1970

THE COLLEGE DISCOVERY PROGRAM

After 10 years in the Public Education System, with 2 years at the 600 school and 8 years at DeWitt Clinton High School, I decided to move onto a new career on the college level. Soon after I resigned from DeWitt Clinton High School in June 1968, I was offered and accepted a position as Director of the newly initiated N.Y. City University experimental program called College Discovery (CD). The program was designed to develop a series of methods to encourage and help economically deprived students attend college.

After I received and accepted that offer for one year as CD Director, I shortly after received a notice from Fordham University that I had applied and been accepted into their pre-doctoral program. I agreed to proceed with both offers concurrently with university classes at night. A very heavy schedule. The Fordham notice stated that once I completed the preliminary twelve credits, I would be eligible for an appointment to Fordham University while working on my Ph.D.

The students in the CD program were recommended to Queensborough Community College (QCC) based on their desire to attend, their potential ability to handle college work and their family income. Students who were admitted to the CD program understood that they were enrolled in a four-year baccalaureate degree transfer program that was not limited to liberal arts. Their education would begin at a community college and then continue at a senior college upon satisfactory completion of the CD requirements.

QCC students were admitted based on their high school records and SAT scores. By contrast, CD students with unsatisfactory high school records and test scores had customarily not been encouraged to apply because they were not considered college material. We later proved in the CD program that being economically deprived did not mean that a student could not succeed in college. This was the basic premise of CD.

My first approach to the CD position was to hire dozens of CD therapists. The ratio of students to therapists was 6 to 1, in order to understand better what was hindering each student. The counselors conferred with the students regularly, did program evaluations, met with the student's instructors, arranged for tutoring and economic support and provided encouragement. The counselors spent all day with the students discussing their needs.

Director Winston Allen holding a faculty meeting
with the CD therapists.

Director Winston Allen holding a faculty meeting
with the CD therapists

As Director of the CD program, soon after arriving on the job in September 1968, I conducted an overall program evaluation, arranged for tutoring and economics and provided encouragement. The climate triggered confrontation between disadvantaged black and Hispanic CD students and white non-CD students and some instructors. At QCC there was tension between CD students and some QCC students on campus, straining the already tenuous relationship between the disadvantaged black and Hispanic CD students and the white non-CD students and faculty at QCC.

Whenever I could, I invited guest speakers to the CD program, such as Joe Davis, who had had deficiencies in his school academic record from Mississippi but later had gone on to have a successful career as an executive search firm CEO working with the Ford Foundation. A speaker, such as Joe Davis, provided his own life experiences with motivational, encouraging stories. The CD students could learn from his personal experiences, overcoming hurdles. I also invited professionals from various vocations to meet with the students to offer encouragement in what I called Career Opportunity Seminars.

I sponsored the program because it often inspired students and gave CD students a view into the lives of many who started out with difficulties which they overcame and went on to great accomplishments. I was able to have as a guest speaker Ossie Davis, who engrossed the students with many of his life experiences. The event was attended by QCC President Schmeller and the QCC students.

Although I felt that in one year, I had not had sufficient time to do all that I wanted to do as CD Director, I was able to institute new programs and approaches that continued after my year ended and I was able to make a difference and help the CD students overcome some of the hurdles that existed in their lives.

It became clear to me that going from the demanding position I had as CD Director to night school at the same time was very exhausting and that I needed to speed up my track to my doctorate, which would give me an opportunity to help more people to overcome the barriers that they had ahead of them. To accelerate my coursework for my

Ph.D. program, I put in my resignation as CD Director effective at the end of the year.

I was immediately brought on the faculty at Fordham University while I worked on my Ph.D. The faculty at Fordham University was very welcoming.

FORDHAM UNIVERSITY

Fordham University needed an experienced person to be an instructor at the Fordham Graduate School at Lincoln Center. In 1969, because of the accelerated civil rights movement, Fordham had decided to offer relevant ethnic studies courses to its master's degree students, soon to be applying for New York City public school teaching jobs. I was asked to prepare and teach two new graduate courses. One was Contemporary Black America and Its Cultural Heritage, and the other was Racism in America. Both courses got good reviews from students and administrators.

Racism in America was hands-on, and one of the sessions involved a lecture at the Schomburg Center in Harlem, a unique research center for black life and history that was a part of the New York City's public library system. The Schomburg Center for Research in Black Culture remains devoted to connecting, preserving and sharing evidence documenting the history and culture of people of African descent.

I indicated to students at the beginning of the semester that their attendance at the lecture was required, and almost all the students attended. The reactions following the visits were particularly interesting. Several graduate students told me that they had been apprehensive about going into Harlem at the time but were ultimately very glad that they had gone to the Schomburg Center. Being from other communities, they had been led to believe that there were no institutions of learning in Harlem that were worthy of their time, and their fear of attack in the 1960's was ever present. At the time, Harlem was 100 percent black, and my students were 100 percent white.

Some students said they were surprised to find all the reading rooms at the Schomburg Center in Harlem crowded with students quietly reading, and to see students studying filmstrips in the video room and youngsters doing their homework after school in the large reading room. At that time, the lifestyle in this inner-city community was not well understood, and many of the Fordham University graduate students said that they were impressed by the serious academic activity at the workshop. I was granted the tenure track position of Assistant Professor.

One student said to me, "In all my undergraduate and graduate classes, I had some very good classes, but nothing matched this course in its poignancy and its clarity of issues. Racism in America had its greatest impact on me because it opened up my eyes for exploring some data and discourse that was not present on college campuses. I strongly support it, and it should be a required course in this graduate school."

During the first year, since Fordham had indicated an interest in innovative teaching strategies, I researched and proposed to Fordham University a unique overseas internship program under the title International Education Institutes Workshop. It would be conducted in the summer when city-wide teachers, administrators and graduate students could attend. The program took an expectant year of planning, and its implementation date was July, 1972.

By that time, I had just been recruited by Xerox as a consultant, and they granted me a four-week leave to conduct the program. In the summer of 1972, I took the group to London and Durham, England and Carmarthen, Wales for Fordham's first internship program for teachers and administrators, formally known as the International Education Institute's Workshop in Open Education, that would be conducted the next summer in London, England and Carmarthen, Wales.

The institute offered Fordham graduate students, as well as selected groups of teachers, administrators and supervisors, a firsthand internship experience with some innovative British teaching approaches that had astounding results in student motivation and results. In this approach, the stylized role of teachers and students was discarded for much freer, highly individualized, student-centered learning.

The Fordham workshop cost, including round-trip transportation to London and from London to Carmarthen, Wales; resident accommodation; breakfast and supper; health and accident insurance; and gratuities, was $1,300. The program sold out almost immediately.

Teaching at Fordham University, although two years, a very brief stay, exceeded my expectations because Fordham was a receptive environment very conducive to scholarship and innovation. I was at Fordham for only two years, but I had brought an additional program to the university that was well received and constituted a new course. I was offered a place on the list of prospects for the Fordham University position as Dean, and although it was a vote of confidence, I knew that with my broker-dealer firm, I would not have time and could not consider the position. I remember my tenure at Fordham as an unexpected but smooth transition in my career.

I have the best memories of Fordham, where I received my Ph.D., which proved essential in my next move to Xerox in 1970. I had received a leave of absence from Fordham University, and my position was kept open for three years until the 1974–1975 semester, when Fordham reluctantly became convinced that I would not be returning from Xerox.

I formally resigned from Fordham University in 1973. My independent broker-dealership with absentee leadership moved along. With great effort from existing representatives and from clients, we had several very good years at Creative during the 1970s. I had completed my Ph.D. at Fordham University and had served two years as Assistant Professor. Throughout my stay at Xerox, which turned out to be ten years, I continued to maintain my company.

I was handling multiple careers for some time with considerable help from my managers and thanks to particularly good leadership including annual audits, with very good results. I knew the base that I had put in place was strong enough to keep my company profitable.

Balancing multiple careers is not for everyone, but for those who can do it, they realize the benefits long after the grueling schedule is a thing of the past. I have often been asked how you managed multiple careers and a business. It is easier when you know that you are working toward achieving what you set out to do.

Chapter 15

My Ten-Year Corporate Executive Experience with Xerox 1971–1981

The front-page *New York Times* photo of me and an article entitled *"Crash Course Creates Salesmen"* published on July 31, 1968 detailing how I had found and trained numerous novice prospects for the Series 7 exam and discussing how they all had passed the challenging registered representative exam and joined my Wall Street firm, caught the eye of the CEO of Xerox Corporation.

Xerox placed an ad in the newspaper to fill a key position and an old friend of mine, Joe Davis, whom I had mentored years before, contacted Xerox and told them he could put them in touch with the person they told him they wanted, Winston Allen. Xerox told Joe that that they wanted me to come in for an interview for the position.

Xerox told Joe that they did not want Joe to reveal the company's name when he spoke to me. As an Executive Search Firm, Joe Davis Associates, with an office on 41st Street in Manhattan, Joe called me. After we talked for a while, Joe told me that a large company was interested in meeting with me.

I told Joe that I would not be able to meet with the company because of my overcrowded schedule, namely my teaching position at Fordham and my investment company, Creative.

Joe continued to call me in order to get me to meet with the company and each time I turned the meeting down. Finally, Joe called me and said that he wasn't supposed to tell me but the company was Xerox and that the CEO had seen my article in *The New York Times* and that Xerox was very insistent that I come in for a meeting. I finally told Joe that he could set up the meeting at Xerox headquarters in Stamford, Connecticut, and I would talk with them, and he did.

I attended the meeting with several Xerox senior executives at their corporate headquarters in Stamford. They talked to me for a couple of hours about the specific methods I would use to handle specific training problems and I gave them detailed ways I would approach each issue.

At the end of the meeting I was asked if I would go as their consultant and spend a week at their training facility in Fort Lauderdale, Florida and give them my critiques. I agreed to take a week off from Fordham and go to Fort Lauderdale.

The Xerox training facility was located at the Sheridan Hotel directly facing the beach in Fort Lauderdale. It was spring break for college students and that was a distraction for everyone as the college students played volleyball and frolicked on the beach just outside the widows.

As I watched the classes I saw immediately that there were major deficiencies in the way the Xerox training program and classes were structured. Many things were wrong. (1) The trainers were talking to the students who were prospective salesmen, about how to sell. (2) Trainers spent a good deal of time telling the students how successful the salesmen had been on sales calls. (3) The students were seated in theatre style seats to listen to the trainer in the front of the room. (4)

Students were supposed to listen and take notes (5) Trainers did most of the talking and the students sat passively, except for occasional questions. (6) The distractions from the volleyball made listening difficult.

These were only some of the most obvious problems that I noted and planned to report to Xerox. I knew that, as was the case for most companies during the 1960s, Xerox theory was that salesmen who had demonstrated their skills in selling Xerox copiers and duplicators should teach others to sell.

In my experience, I had found that great salespeople were usually poor teachers and that their war-stories heralding their great successes did not help trainees learn how to acquire the necessary skills. I informed all involved that it was essential that sales training be interactive so that sales staff could learn how best to handle customers' questions and concerns.

Also, salespeople in any company, especially a 80 billion dollar corporation, needed to practice and perfect their techniques for selling benefits and meeting customers objections. In order to do this, salespeople had to be able to identify their customer's needs, be able to read their prospective customers and answer their questions precisely.

In my week observing classes in their training program there was very little I observed that I found effective. Particularly lecturing to students interspersed with a string of their successful "war stories." This type of training could not produce the results that Xerox needed and wanted. In short, their training methods needed a major overhaul to become effective.

Back in Xerox corporate headquarters in Stamford, I met with the top decision makers. As I began my report that afternoon, the conference room was quiet as I presented my findings, conclusions and recommendations. The only sound aside from my voice was their pencils against long yellow pads, taking notes.

I told them sales training at Xerox at that time was not interactive but needed to be. Videotaped role-playing, an inter-active tool for sales training had not been utilized at Xerox. It was most essential so that sales staff could learn the techniques of handling customer questions and concerns. Also, salespeople needed to practice and perfect their techniques for selling benefits and meeting objectives.

Following my presentation and report I was offered the job of heading up the entire training and development function at Xerox. I turned down the offer of a full-time position at that time but indicated I would consider continuing as a consultant as I was still on the faculty of Fordham, on a leave of absence.

With my decision about to be made, I checked out the details of the offer, weighing my options as I saw them. I talked to friends and family about my decision. Not surprisingly, I got several negative reactions: "Corporations are cutthroat operations. You're in a very good position at Fordham. Why subject yourself to the whims of a corporation?"

These considerations, while they may have been valid, did not get to the nexus of the issue: this was an opportunity to enter a multi-billion-dollar corporation in a senior management position. I phoned Xerox a week later as promised and accepted their office for a six-month period until I could wrap up my faculty position at Fordham.

For several months, my staff and I worked around the clock. After setting stringent goals for our group, I held out for tests in the field as a measurement of our effectiveness, During that period, I instituted the first teacher-training program. This new area I called "Train the Trainer," which provided a crash course in training methodology.

Within weeks of my taking the position, I pulled together a permanent staff of professionals who were able to get the training restructuring introduced throughout the corporation. I devised the overall strategy, including the process, for training sales and technical personnel. The thirty professionals that I recruited and hired were equipped to do curriculum development, instructor training, audiovisual technology and curriculum evaluation.

This was a great asset to me because the Xerox training facility was in the final stages of completion and I had committed to having the program in place when the new facility opened. Many of the people that I hired came from earlier professional relationships, and I knew that they could get the job done.

To assess the success of my operation and its innovative approach, an audit was ordered by Xerox CEO, Peter McColough, and conducted by Xerox Learning Systems (XLS). Xerox wanted to be certain that they had invested in the right approach, and my strategy for training thousands of Xerox people. Their audit, dated March 1973, called our program "very successful." This was great news for me and my staff, because it meant that we had effectively transformed Xerox training that would be institutionalized.

The most important acceptance made to me by Xerox was their written agreement allowing me to keep Creative operational and active while

I was employed at Xerox. This was an unusual concession because corporations almost never allow their executives to engage in outside business ventures, citing dual loyalties and conflicting interests.

We agreed on the terms and I was given a set of offices at the Xerox temporary corporate headquarters at High Ridge Park in Stamford, Connecticut while the permanent corporate headquarters nearby was being completed, and we moved there. I immediately began to recruit a per diem staff of professionals who I knew would be able to begin systematically addressing the necessary changes in the Xerox Training system.

I insisted on quality results, and I did not renew short-term engagements if production was not forthcoming. For several months, my staff and I worked around the clock. At the same time, we had to adopt logical and operational strategies for responding to requests for training assistance from the field training groups. After setting goals for our group, I held out for tests in the field as a measure of our effectiveness.

In addition to a complete overall of the way training was done at Xerox, I instituted the first formal teacher-training program. This new area I called "Train the Trainer," which proved a crash course in training methodology. Keeping with my philosophy of continuing education, teacher trainers and trainees received home-study modules for training in the classroom and use on the job. Trainers would give the trainees an opportunity to develop their sales skills and techniques in order to close the deal.

The state-of-the art high-tech living and learning center had rooms for over a thousand students at any one time. It was on a two thousand two hundred sixty five acre site. My boss, Bill Duetting was in charge of the hotel facility and I was in charge of the learning part of the facility. On June 2, 1973, Xerox Word dedicated an entire issue to the Leesburg Center, that was very supportive of our program.

Throughout my entire stay at Leesburg I chose to live in Maryland. I had purchased a one story home on River Road in Bethesda, Maryland. It turned out to be a location that impacted me and also the Director of the Leesburg facility, Virginia who lived 60 miles away in Mc Clean, Virginia and was told by the CEO to pick me up at my home each morning and drive me home each day.

This directive was given for at least three reasons, for safety in the early 1970's, traveling on the thruways alone, to provide staff with awareness of my constant visible support from upper management. This continued for the entire three years that I was at Leesburg. In August of 1975 I was promoted to Corporate Headquarters in Stamford Connecticut. This all became clearer to me one evening at a Social of executives: and my wife said to the Director's wife,

"Poor, Win" and she responded "Poor Win, Poor Bill!"

Evidently Bill's wife was reacting to the difficulty Bill had traveling long distances to pick me up and drop me off each day.

Xerox World/Special Section

The Center in Leesburg

On June 2, The Xerox International Center for Training and Management Development opened its doors to its first students—some 400 Xerox sales and service people.

The Leesburg Center is the culmination of a Xerox dream to offer the very best training and development programs to its people.

When the center is in high gear, technical representatives, sales representatives, computer scientists, managers—more than a thousand students at a time—will be educated in its elaborate facilities on a 2,265-acre site in rural Leesburg, Va.

This special section of *Xerox World* is devoted to the Leesburg Center—its history, its philosophy, its reality and its future.

---

erox World

Leesburg: A Xerox Commitment to the Development of Its People

By Mandi Harris

Research in Education

'Xerox has always had a commitment o people development," said Dr. Winston Allen. "This center is the ultimate. Here we have the opportunity to be the pioneers in industrial training."

And if Xerox is the pioneer, Allen could be called the wagon master. He is the Leesburg Center's manager of education research and development.

This department works side by side with the Rochester curriculum group and the Center's school managers. They decide what is to be taught, and Allen's group works out with them the best ways to teach it.

Allen and his staff are in-house experts on how people learn. They bring to the Center the latest knowhow in behavioral science, research, curriculum and instructional technology. They determine the best method of instruction for particular courses, and provide structure for the training programs. "In other words," said Allen, "we define the best way to get the message across."

Very often that method is visual. It has been found that people learn best through seeing and doing. So interaction plays an important part in the Center's training programs. The idea is to make the classroom experience as close to real life as possible.

"That's why there is a lot of importance placed on the role-playing technique," Allen said. "These role-plays are videotaped and replayed by the students; they learn by watching themselves and correcting their mistakes.

"We have used videotaping in previous training schools," Allen said, "but not to the degree that it is used here at Leesburg."

The octagon-shaped classroom is another innovation in education strategy, Allen said. It is based on the concept of give-and-take between the instructor and student, and between student and student.

"They learn from each other as well as from the instructor," he said. "The lecture process isn't as effective largely because the students play a very passive role. In our program they're very active. The more active the students are, the more they learn."

The very idea of a Leesburg Center—in which students from all over the country come to one place to pursue several disciplines—extends beyond the classroom by giving students a chance to see what is on the other side of the fence, to learn to appreciate business disciplines other than their own.

"Through this interaction", said Allen, "the students become better aware of the direction of the company, which in turn fosters professional growth and development.

"Here we can test new teaching methods, new media, and new techniques for introducing multi-media into the curriculum. We can further develop and implement our own research designs to further enhance our training products. This center is second to none in capabilities and potential."

In its short existence, the Center has already been visited by interest groups ranging from Army training specialists to Harvard University professors. It's entirely possible, said Allen, that instructional techniques developed at Leesburg will eventually be adopted by traditional learning institutions.

"And we're working closely with several colleges and universities," he said, "with an eye toward developing accredited programs here for our own people—courses in business administration, educational technology and psychology."

Dr. Winston Allen, Leesburg's manager of education research and development, heads a staff he hopes will pioneer in education technique.

121

Winston at his desk at Leesburg

Winston at Leesburg

Another facet of my expanded assignment was professional service in the community, another of my corporate responsibilities. Xerox corporate executive officer (CEO) Peter McColough wanted executives to seek out experiences in the larger community, such as university affiliations and membership on boards of directors. I was offered a position as adjunct professor of management sciences at the graduate business school at George Washington University and American University, where I served for several semesters. I also accepted speaking engagements at a number of community and business organizations. I was also appointed to a position as a member of the board of directors for the United States Committee for United Nations International Children's Education Fund (UNICEF), where I served on the board for ten years between 1972 and 1982. UNICEF's mission was to work to meet the needs of the world's children. Harry Belafonte, singer and entertainer, became the UNICEF corporate director during my ten-year tenure. Serving on UNICEF's board was fulfilling because the organization financed projects on behalf of the welfare of children throughout the world.

I also served as a member on the board of directors of the National Advisory Council on Minorities in Engineering (NACME), which was a national organization designed to bring about a tenfold increase in the number of minority engineering graduates within the next decade.

I also had a role in working with the Xerox Palo Alto Research Center (PARC) in Palo Alto, California. A great experience for me with a group of scientists in the computer world. Created in 1970, PARC's mission was long-term research in computer science and electronics. Researchers probed the frontier of integrated circuitry, artificial intelligence and laser beams.

The people of the suit-and-tie shirt culture at Rochester's Xerox manufacturing center had a tough time dealing with the T-shirt culture of the beanbag-chair-sitting nerds at PARC. We had a roomful of beanbag chairs on the floor surrounded by circular blackboards.

Throughout its early years, PARC had fifty-eight of the world's top one hundred computer scientists under one roof, and any one of them could have become a leader in the intellectual technical industry. Their featured products were a pointing device (a mouse), overlapping windows, a black-on-white screen and graphic capability.

My job was to set up presentations for the Intellectual Technology (IT) people in the Bay Area and beyond. Steve Jobs and Bill Gates were steady visitors, and they soaked up ideas that they could apply for their future products and concepts. Xerox did not believe in the new computer age and was not prepared to market IT products since IT was a fledgling industry in 1970, when I arrived. Hence, Xerox missed out on an entire industry, one in which they were ahead of other corporations. Xerox at that time could dabble in IT because they were loaded with money from their monopoly business, copiers and duplicators, which simply poured money into the coffers. At one point Xerox executives were not permitted to fly other than first class. I remember being stuck in Barcelona for an extra day because no first-class seats were available on a flight back home.

Outsiders considered PARC to be one of the finest basic research centers in the United States, if not the world. Xerox had the same problem with PARC that AT&T had with Bell Laboratories: getting good ideas to the marketplace. Too many things escaped to other companies. PARC technology, for example, wound up in Apple's Lisa and Macintosh computers. PARC was only one of my responsibilities. I had a basic job of introducing innovations into the Xerox's system of training all its employees, including salespeople, servicemen and managers.

Peter McColough became chief executive officer in 1968, very close to the date when I began at Xerox. He held that position for eighteen years. During the time he was CEO, revenues went from $739 million to $8.5 billion. Peter McColough was a mentor who had selected me for the firm based largely on the article he had read in *The New York Times* back on July 31, 1968. I joined Xerox in 1970 without seeking out the job but by being recruited based on Peter's lead. Xerox grew to $14 billion and some might say Peter was in the right place at the right time. I could be described in the same way because my success was related to both hard work and luck, and I was in the right place at the right time.

When I began my career as a Xerox executive, my intuition told me that no act of kindness could obscure the fact that some at Xerox might be opposed to my presence for a number of reasons. For example, I knew some might be unhappy that I was coming in at a high level with the possibility of proposing changes that could affect them or their job security. This was another hurdle that I needed to be aware of and overcome.

I also recognized that most of the employees at Xerox had not had experience with a black management person, so I could expect some sort of reaction to the position I held. The resistance was covert because it was known that I had earned the confidence of the senior management team at Xerox. Xerox's CEO Peter McColough ordered an audit of my entire operation after I had been on the job six months to assess the success of my operation and its innovative approach. The audit, dated March 1973, called my program "very successful." This was great news for me and my staff because it meant that we had effectively transformed Xerox's methods, enabling them to be institutionalized. The audit circulated in the corporation, detailing the very productive results that my department had achieved.

As the audit circulated, it legitimized the investment that Xerox had made in me. The audit quickly led to greater requests for my services throughout the company. My program was then taken to Rank Xerox operations in London and Europe; the Palo Alto Research Center in Stamford, California; and the Scientific Data System in Dallas, Texas.

This experience at Xerox illustrated to me the essentials of building wealth by using some of it for investment purposes. Those who want to one day run their own show should know that corporate America turned out to be a very good training ground for me. Everything that was included in my nine-to-five job was also preparing me for opportunity. I was fortunate to be part of a Fortune 50 corporation with international responsibilities because I could use my widespread knowledge to further my next entrepreneurial effort.

After three years, in September 1975, I received a commendation and was moved to corporate headquarters on High Ridge Road in Stamford, Connecticut. I was given an expanded assignment, including work with Rank Xerox, a European arm of the company. I was to work with Rank Xerox in Dusseldorf, Germany. Once there, I found that they were receptive. I then made a follow-up trip to Rank Xerox in London, England.

I got notice from Xerox headquarters in October 1975 that I had completed my assignment in Leesburg, Virginia, after three years and I was being moved to corporate headquarters to assume a new responsibility that would have me traveling internationally. During that three-year period, I overcame many hurdles and had been very successful with my assignment. The barriers included the corporate racism at Xerox in Leesburg, Virginia.

I was ready to relocate from Bethesda, Maryland, where I had been living for the past three years while working at Leesburg. My first overseas trip would be to Dusseldorf, Germany, to meet with senior management of the training operation. I put my house up for sale in Bethesda and found a house in Connecticut. I decided to look at Westport, Connecticut, an attractive coastal suburb thirty minutes from Xerox corporate headquarters in Stamford, Connecticut, where I would be working.

My wife, Ruby, and I were traveling through Westport after a Labor Day weekend in New Jersey with friends. We decided to stop at a real estate firm. I was driving. As she thumbed through the real estate section of *The New York Times,* Ruby said, "Here is a firm, the Edith Davidson Real Estate Company. Why not go in here?"

We did as she had suggested. The salesperson behind the desk greeted us with a cordial "Hello. How can we help you?"

I said "I will be heading up a function in the personnel department at Xerox corporate headquarters in Stamford, and we are interested in finding a house in Westport."

Someone from the back office shouted, "He's from Xerox. Send him in here!" That was when Edith Davidson introduced herself as the owner of the firm. Ruby and I found ourselves meeting with a woman who would change our life completely.

Edith wasted no time. She said, "I have been trying to get my relocation business going with Xerox, and I constantly have difficulty from someone on the inside. Now I could have a friend in the Xerox corporate office."

"What kind of house are you looking for?" Without hesitation I described our dream house: ultramodern design, architecturally deluxe, and near water. Edith Davidson thumbed through her Rolodex and said, "I have a house that I believe you're going to love. Let's go."

Little did I know that she was taking us to one of the most spectacular houses in Connecticut that we would be living in for almost fifty years. Edith drove us to the only house we ever visited in Westport that day. We went over to 4 Burritts Landing North, with a sign as you entered the area: Burritts Landing North, Private.

The house was an ultramodern glass house. I knew immediately this was our dream house and we would need to move fast because we did not want any slipups. I said to Ruby, "This is it. Let's go." I said to Edith, "I have a flight to Bethesda, Maryland, where we live, so I'll call you in the morning."

At 9:00 AM the next day, I called Edith Davidson. I said, "I'm ready to wire my deposit to you." My deposit was one-third of the asking price of $142,500. Edith said, "I could see that you really liked it." I wired the amount of $47,500 and waited a short time for her to call telling me that she had received my wire and the house was ours. It came within a few hours. Ruby and I celebrated.

The house was all glass with thirty floor-to-ceiling glass windows. It had natural stone walls outside and inside; cherrywood floors through the main wing with a living room; a natural stone fireplace; a master bedroom; a kitchen; a dining room; an office; and two baths.

All this overlooked a picturesque spring-fed half-acre pond near a cantilevered seventy-five-foot deck. The other side of the house had its own radiant heat system under stone floors with two bedrooms, a separate kitchen and bath and a two-car garage. A week later we closed on the house, then I took off for Dusseldorf, Germany.

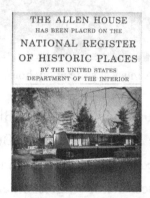

U.S. Department of the Interior "Landmarked House"

The architects drawing of the landmarked "Allen House"

A musical soire at my home

In addition to the unusual architecture, Roy Binkley protégé of Mies Van der Rohe was the architect and the 4 Burritts Landing North landscape was designed by Frank Okamura (1912–2006), who had lost his gardening business in Los Angeles when he, his wife, and their daughters were interned in the Manzanar Relocation Camp for the duration of World War II. He had become the curator of the Brooklyn Botanical Japanese Garden and took on special commissions, one of which was our property.

This house represents the only example of Binkley's work in Connecticut. When this modern house became eligible in 2008, because it was over fifty years old, which was the requisite period needed, it was awarded a Connecticut preservation designation in 2009. I then applied for the National Register. The Secretary of the Interior, acting through the National Park Service, has the power to survey, document, evaluate, acquire and preserve archeological and historic sites throughout the country. The Allen House was designated a historical home.

The current landscaping with features of waterfalls was designed by me. Because of this new introduction, my interest was sparked in Japanese gardens. I signed up and took courses at the Bronx Botanical Gardens to enable me to re-create the gardens that would best fit the property. The Allen House has been placed on the National Register of Historic Places by the United States Department of the Interior.

Ruby and I were delighted when we discovered the other features of the purchase: private area, community Olympic-size swimming pool, and a beach and a dock for all owners who lived in Burritts Landing. A few neighbors told me that they had all received a letter from the Edith Davidson Real Estate Firm informing them that they should not be concerned that the house had been sold to a black couple, as she wanted them to know, Dr. Allen was an executive at Xerox Corporation in Stamford.

One of my neighbors told me: "You overpaid for your house. Moderns are not selling, and the house had been on the market for some time." How important to find that I had an opportunity to encourage modern architectural thinking in Westport, Connecticut, something that was stifled out in Germany when the Bauhaus school of modern architecture was driven out by the Nazi regime. The property is greatly admired now and featured in articles about modern architecture in magazines and newspapers.

By the time I returned from Europe, Xerox had completed the move from Bethesda. I never even got to see my previous home again. I discovered when I returned that my Westport house had been built by the architect Roy Binkley from the renowned Mies van der Rohe school of architecture in Chicago.

This was my introduction to the many wonders of that particular school of architecture, the Bauhaus school, which was the most celebrated art school of modern times. It was closed down by the Berlin police, acting on instructions of the new Nazi government, on April 11, 1933. That was a tangible expression of the Nazi Party's cultural policy, of its determination to remove from Germany every trace of what it called "decadent" and "Bolshevistic" art.

In the early 1980's American corporations were adopting sharp cost-cutting budgets and reducing power on a permanent basis by outsourcing as a result of globalization. In July 1981, many small consulting firms had begun to market their training programs to major corporations. Many large companies were also looking to farm out their training needs to outside firms. To reduce costs, training was a ripe area.

About this time, I was ready to leave Xerox. I had several offers, in addition to a Xerox offer for another assignment, but I decided that after ten years with Xerox, and Peter McColough's retiring I should move on.

I was looking forward to taking Creative in a new direction. It is so important to always look many years ahead. I decided to add another product line to my business and I started a real estate syndication company, Equity Properties, Ltd.

By delegating the day-to-day operations, Creative continued throughout my tenure with Xerox. What lay ahead were real estate syndications and private placements.

Winston in Dusseldorf Germany at Xerox

Winston in Dusseldorf, Germany at Xerox

Winston in Dusseldorf, Germany at Xerox

Rank Xerox headquarters in Dusseldorf, Germany. Winston Allen with
Rank Xerox executive discussing staff development strategies, 1976.

Dr. Herkens & Dr. Allen
RANK XEROX HEADQUARTERS
Dusseldorf, Germany
July 1972

Conclusion of Meeting at Xerox in Dusseldorf, Germany - 1976

Chapter 16

My Experience Syndicating Deluxe Co-Op Manhattan Apartments, 1983–1986

As a securities broker-dealer and real estate broker my company was ideally structured to purchase blocks of Manhattan apartments and secure investors for the syndication of deluxe apartments in Manhattan.

The premise was that Equity Properties would get a discount from what the price would have been if the apartment had been vacant. The discounts ranged up to about 50 percent of market value. If the tenant moved out quickly Equity Properties reaped a windfall, if not the company would hope to cover part of the costs with rents.

Investors who were prospects for purchasing an interest in the packaged apartments through Equity Properties would become subject to the New York City rent-stabilization laws regarding tenant rights. They would be responsible for supplementing any shortfalls between the rents received from the rent-stabilized tenants and the co-op maintenance and other related expenses.

Equity Properties was now servicing clients with marketing investments and real estate products as I expanded to a new product line to offer to them. The time was right in 1982 in New York City because there were thousands of deluxe New York City apartment conversions from rentals to co-ops, and thousands of rental tenants were given the option of purchasing their apartments and becoming shareholders in New York City.

Under the rent stabilization law, tenants who chose not to purchase could continue to rent their apartments and legally remain there for the rest of their lives. The apartments that were not purchased by the occupying tenants could be purchased by my investors. The term unsold shares refer to those shares of the co-op corporation that were not purchased by tenants who occupied the units at the time the property was converted from a rental property to cooperative ownership.

The lure that attracted my investors to buy these apartments was prices 50 percent to 70 percent below market value. This was an opportunity to overcome barriers, hurdles and obstacles in upscale sections of Manhattan in which my investors could not find residences. I used my broker-dealer credentials and connections and my real estate broker's license to form a syndication.

My company purchased the occupied apartments that had not been purchased by occupying tenants as unsold shares to investors, mainly in blocks of six for management efficiency. The investors shared the rental income, expenses, depreciation and tax deductions. *The New York Times* ran an article about me in the real estate section on Sunday, December 2, 1984.

The investors in unsold shares of tenant-occupied prime New York City co-op apartments could derive substantial benefits from three factors: appreciation in value, cash flow and tax advantages. The investors became subject to the New York City rent stabilization laws regarding tenant rights. They became responsible for the shortfall between the rents received from the rent-stabilized tenants and the co-op maintenance and other related expenses until the tenant vacated the apartment and the apartment could be rented or sold at market value.

Since the syndication was being sold as a tax shelter as well as a long-term appreciating asset, investors needed a legal exception from the IRS stating that the IRS would honor the specified terms of the tax shelter that I had structured. I located a highly reputable Wall Street law firm, Brown, Wood, Ivey, Mitchell & Petty, that agreed to do the very expensive legal work for me pro bono, so that I could offer the unsold shares for sale with the tax benefits. Their pro bono agreement resulted from our realization that the cost of their legal services would kill the deal. Moreover, in the future, they could use my syndication model, once it was granted, for future business.

The City Trust Bank in Connecticut saw the potential of financing prime Manhattan real estate in the mid-1980s and provided me with financing of my syndication. My presentation and the timing were evidently just right because I received a $2 million check from City Trust Bank in two days. The purchase agreement to exercise my option to buy the unsold share apartments or units stipulated a limited time for me to do so. The next step to close the deal was my completion of an offering memorandum and obtaining financing, which I put in place at that time by using other people's money.

When the market for tax-sheltered real estate syndications dropped off following the new Tax Reform Act of 1986, which eliminated the tax benefit, one of the three benefits of ownership of unsold shares, my investors sold their ownership, and I purchased many of the apartments for myself from investors who wanted to cash out.

A few years after my purchase, the Manhattan real estate market turned around and the appreciation of these unsold share units as investments increased sharply.

The takeaway from my experience was that creative ideas may be the door to wealth-building. Since the opportunity was viable, I took the risk and made my purchase. Successful people capitalize on smart opportunities that others are reluctant to pursue. Sometimes the inability to seize a seemingly viable opportunity is the result of the fear that it is too difficult to accomplish or unwillingness to gain the knowledge required to go forward.

Unsold Share Duplex Apartments on Madison Avenue, New York City

Chapter 17

My Two Inventions: Hydrotherapy (HydroTone) and Water Purification (WaterProtec)

HYDROTHERAPY

My invention, and later the patented product, which I called HydroTone was designed to deliver pressurized water to any part of the body. The product in the home shower will do what a whirlpool or Jacuzzi tub does, but it is portable and can be used as often as wanted and the temperature can be changed from hot-to-cold with ease. I patented my invention, a grant gives the inventor the right to exclude others from, making, using or selling the invention throughout the U.S. for a period of twenty years. I had produced the only portable hydrotherapy single-stream jet water shower massager.

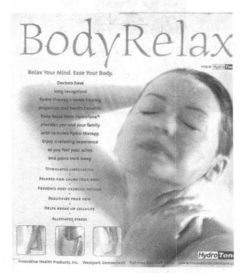

My invention

Presenting my invention to Johnnie Cochran

I had an idea and ended up with a patented product. It all began when my wife sustained a shoulder sprain when helping to dock our boat. She had tried many different remedies for her pain without much relief. The Jacuzzi with its 40 to 85 pounds per inch (ppi) pressure jet was good, but it was only helpful when it could be used outdoors in warm weather. I had the idea that I could fashion a portable device to simulate the effects of a Jacuzzi that could be used in our home shower whenever you wished. The portable pressurized water device could be applied to any area of the body that was in pain to gain relief. I developed a prototype of my idea, and it was effective with my wife's shoulder pain. She was able to realize the effects of a Jacuzzi or whirlpool but in the home shower every day without the unnecessary expense or time required for a Jacuzzi.

Conversing with HydroTone Customers

Demonstrating my invention at Medi-Spa Trade Show

Physicians have long recognized hydrotherapy, the use of water, to enhance health, increase circulation and give relief from muscle pain. Hydrotherapy, a unique way to use nature's oldest medicine—water—benefits the entire body and can be used in a variety of ways without side effects to help control acute conditions. I decided to patent and market my invention.

As I looked through the patent rules and regulations, I found them to be overwhelming. But I concluded that it was not cost-effective for me to engage a patent attorney at the start. I headed down the complex road of the patent process on my own. After several office actions requiring answers to questions by the patent examiner and my responses, I finally received the patent.

The entire process, from the first submission for the utility patent, to the patent office's response, to the waiting period to submit, to obtaining both the utility patent and the design patent, took four years. By obtaining the patent, I had produced the only portable hydrotherapy single-stream jet water shower massager.

The next step was to develop a product. That would be risky, although people who take risks tend to be the achievers. Long-term thinkers look ahead to possible long-term payoffs. They see risk-taking as the doorway to success, and for them, the higher the risk, the more exciting the venture. I had an engineer build the prototype, and the product was manufactured in the U.S. rather than in China or another foreign country for production.

To market my HydroTone, Body Relax, invention, I went on the road to demonstrate the product. I market-tested HydroTone by going into the field and having people try the product and respond to questions about it. Once we saw that there was overwhelming interest in having and purchasing the product, I took it to trade shows; shopping networks like QVC, where we appeared; and catalogues for online shoppers and had success with the marketing of HydroTone.

Winston E. Allen, Ph.D.

WATER PURIFICATION

I studied tap water conditions in Westport, Connecticut while I served as Chairman of the Westport, Conservation Commission for five years, a voluntary Town appointed position. I conducted tests of the well water on Westport properties and found that the water had numerous chemical impurities that needed to be removed.

I decided to continue my study of water purification needs after I moved on to another Town of Westport voluntary position, namely The Zoning Board of Appeals (ZBA) for 24 years. To address the problem of water purification in tap water in the Westport homes, I formed a company whose mission was to develop a system for removing chemical contaminants from household water.

I named my company *WaterProtec*. I produced a whole house water purification system that I sold to homeowners who use it to this day in numerous homes in Westport. The business was very successful and would have continued, if I could have put the time required that was precluded by my many other business obligations. The demand continues to this day. Many households and past customers use bottled water as a substitute for their drinking water. However, it cannot replace the water source of purified water for bathing and other household uses in the home.

WATERPR⬡TEC®

Protect your family's health with Waterprotec®...Water the way it should be

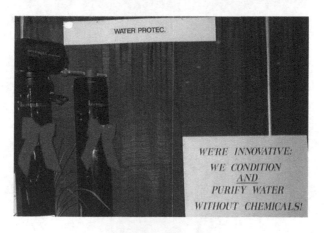

WATER PROTEC.

WE'RE INNOVATIVE:
WE CONDITION
AND
PURIFY WATER
WITHOUT CHEMICALS!

My Water Purification invention

PART IV

Civil Rights Movement, 1920-1968

Chapter 18

Powerless segregated Businesses—1921

The first black investment firm that sprung up was not in New York City in the 1960's but in Tulsa, Oklahoma in the 1920's. Every segregated city in the U.S. in the post–Civil War period had one thriving black business. Each thriving black business was created and fed upon by segregation and Jim Crow laws. This was one of the consequences of segregation following the Civil-War.

In the U.S., the most successful of the black business districts was in Tulsa, Oklahoma, in the Greenwood section officially known to black America as "Black Wall Street." On May 31, 1921, the thirty-five-block area, that blacks who owned businesses had created had an unprecedented ten black millionaires and as many as six hundred black families in Tulsa at the time each with assets as high as $500,000. In today's dollars that equals $6,621,925.00.

Black families bought food at black-owned grocery stores, bought their clothes at black garment shops and got their shoes fixed by a black shoemaker. Because of segregation laws, they had visitors who stayed in boardinghouses, socialized in black-owned pool halls and bars, and got their hair done at black salons. It was a completely independent black economy. Black families also had their health checked by black doctors, and when necessary, they sued each other with the help of black law firms. They also lived in houses built by black contractors and deposited checks at black-run banks. One of the consequences of the Civil-Right's desegregation movement, on the other hand, was the loss of post-Civil War Black Wall Streets.

In 1921 racism led to the disappearance of Tulsa's black business district. In May 1921, in what is known as the Tulsa race massacre thousands of whites stormed Greenwood, destroying everything in their path. Hundreds of blacks were shot, burned alive or tied to cars and dragged to their death. The City of Tulsa now admits belatedly that it helped fuel the destruction by deputizing lynch mobs. By the time the violence ended, hundreds of blacks had been murdered and the Greenwood section of Tulsa had been completely destroyed.

Examining the history of the city of Tulsa led me to the background data with knowledge of the first "Black Wall Street" story. "By 1921, fueled by oil money, Tulsa had become a growing, prosperous city with a population of more than 100,000 people." Tulsa was also a highly segregated city. Most of the city's ten thousand black residents lived in the Greenwood neighborhood. According to a later Red Cross estimate, some 1,256 houses were burned, while 215 others were looted. Two newspapers, a school, a library, a hospital, churches, hotels, stores and many other black-owned businesses were among the buildings destroyed or damaged by fire.

This factual story, yet obscured, was distressing to me as a teacher of U.S. history in an acclaimed New York City high school. The massacre was totally omitted from the curriculum, the text and the classroom discussion material, as were other atrocities throughout the country. I have a hope that this collective stain on black economic development will not be dismissed from our historical memory. This omission was also true of the school system in Tulsa.

Historically, the normal risks of business were exceeded by the overwhelming violence of an uncontrolled mob and the City of Tulsa supported the mob that resorted to aggression against defenseless people. A takeaway for me was that wealth without power can result in victimization of the powerless. This episode in the U.S. was a precursor to the Holocaust in Europe less than twenty years later. The amnesia permitted us to erase this episode from the history books and our minds in the U.S. public schools.

Arguably, had attention been paid to the slaughter of innocent people because of resentment of their financial success, possibly the Holocaust could have been thwarted. One of the reasons why I resigned from my teaching of American history position in the 1960's was that schools nationwide had eliminated and omitted black history from the curriculum. They simply erased it from any memory, thereby pretending it did not occur.

The Oklahoma State Department of Education under pressure finally required that the topic be taught in Oklahoma history classes beginning in 2000 and U.S. history classes beginning in 2004. The documented story has been included in Oklahoma history books since 2009, and though the dialogue about the reasons and effects of the terms riot vs. massacre is very important, the feelings of those who experienced this devastation, as well as the interpretation of current area residents and historians, have led to a more appropriate name: the 1921 Race Massacre Commission.

This important piece of history affected me directly. The massacre of an entire self-sufficient community was not included in the curriculum for U.S. history students when I taught at DeWitt Clinton

High School in the 1960s, although I added it in my history classes. It was also added throughout the department. This experience was an underlying reason for me to want to gravitate towards a New York Wall Street.

Chapter 19

Brown v. Board of Education, 1954

From the beginning of the 1950's the Civil Rights Movement was at the precipice of a decades-long struggle whose goal was to enforce the constitutional and legal rights for blacks that were already enjoyed by white Americans throughout the South and the remainder of the country. This was but five years after my train ride through the South in 1946. With roots that dated back to the Reconstruction era, from 1865 to 1877 and Jim Crow, the Civil Rights Movement was now about to achieve its largest legislative gains in the late 1950s and mid-1960s. The struggle was about to bear fruit from years of direct action and grassroots protests that were organized from the mid-1950s until 1968.

Encompassing strategies in the 1960s, various groups would come to organize social movements to accomplish the goals of ending legalized racial segregation, disenfranchisement and discrimination in the U.S. I had experienced a taste of this, in my trip through the South in 1946. But the struggles were just beginning, and the outcome was far from certain. In 1951, a plaintiff named Oliver Brown filed a class action suit against the Board of Education of Topeka, Kansas, after his daughter, Linda Brown, was refused entrance to Topeka, Kansas, all-white and segregated elementary schools.

In his lawsuit, Brown asserted that schools for black children were not equal to the schools for white children. He further stated that segregation violated the so-called "equal protection clause" of the

Fourteenth Amendment, which holds that no state can "deny to any person within its jurisdiction the equal protection of the laws." In 1954 the Supreme Court's landmark decision in Brown v. Board of Education resulted from the NAACP's effective legal strategy against segregated education. Blacks gained the formal, if not the practical, right to study alongside white children in public schools. The Brown decision did not achieve school desegregation on its own, and the steadfast resistance to Brown v. Board of Education continued.

This case, which was decided by the Supreme Court of the United States, has had as great an impact upon American life as any other legal decision in U.S. history. It has remained a source of contention and commentary for generations to come. The conditions, mental, physical and legal, that prevailed in the South, in which such a decision came to be, reveal its historic nature. The decision fueled an intransigent, violent resistance during which southern states used a variety of tactics and strategies to evade the law. As a follow-up to *the Brown v. Board of Education* decision, Georgia passed legislation requiring the closing of public schools that had been forced to integrate. The court then ordered their conversion to private schools.

Sixty-seven years after Brown v. Board of Education, very sizable inequities persist in the nation's public-school systems, largely based on residential patterns and disparities in resources between economically disadvantaged districts and wealthy districts. The debate is long from ending as to how to combat the disparities. The movement, using major nonviolent campaigns, would eventually secure new recognition in federal law and federal protection for black America.

Chapter 20

Rosa Parks, Mother of the Civil Rights Movement, 1955

Under segregation, whites were granted the legal right to sit in the larger designated area starting in the front of each bus. The white area was off-limits to all black people no matter the age and the infirmity. The black area could not be expanded, even when the white area was almost empty. Blacks were legally restricted to a limited area in the rear of all buses and public vehicles in all southern states until 1956.

Throughout the South, after blacks paid their fare, even in the worst rainy weather, blacks were required to disembark and re-enter the bus through the back door. They could only hope that the bus driver would not drive away and leave them stranded as they walked outside to the back of the bus or waited on the street for the back door to open.

In 1955, Rosa Parks, sitting on a seat in the white section, refused to give up her seat and move to the back of a bus in Montgomery, Alabama, for which act she was arrested. Rosa Parks was charged with a violation of chapter 5, section 11, the segregation law of the Montgomery City Code. Parks, when she spoke of the devastating incident to her friends, said, "It was the very last time that I was going to ride in humiliation." Park's refusal was a strategic form of nonviolent protest that directly drew dramatic attention to the Civil Rights Movement and showed to the world how vicious and inhumane segregation laws were in Alabama and all other southern states. Her arrest led to the Montgomery bus boycott and to other boycotts.

During the boycott, blacks chose to walk to work. Some traveled twenty miles or more, and some shared cars. Others rode black-operated taxis, which charged only 10¢ per trip, the standard price of a bus fare. The Montgomery bus boycott continued for 381 days and ended only when the City of Montgomery, Alabama, repealed its segregation, which led to massive changes in the entire transportation system and laws throughout the United States. Dr. Martin Luther King Jr. (MLK), local minister of the Dexter Avenue Baptist Church, who had recently moved to Montgomery, was elected to lead the Montgomery Improvement Association. This organization had been set up to expand the boycott efforts against Jim Crow segregation laws in Montgomery. Led by MLK, the movement grew exponentially.

On June 13, 1956, the district court of Montgomery, Alabama, ruled that the enforced segregation of black and white passengers on buses operating in the city of Montgomery violated the Constitution and the laws of the United States because the conditions deprived people of "equal rights under the law." The court further enjoined the state of Alabama "from continuing to operate segregated buses in 1956." Rosa Parks soon became the symbol of the resulting Montgomery bus boycott that immediately erupted, leading her to receive national attention and publicity. She was hailed as the "mother of the Civil Rights Movement."

However, the no. 2857 bus was left unattended and abandoned for years because of this incident in which Rosa Parks was arrested. The bus is now exhibited in the Henry Ford Museum in Dearborn, Michigan. The restoration conservators determined that today's visitors can actually board the bus and sit in Rosa Park's seat and all other seats. The actual bus and not simply an exhibit behind glass is there. The rewards of searching and opening up history are immense. The curator of the museum stated, "I'm still struck by the emotional response that people have after experiencing sitting in Rosa Park's actual seat from 1955. Many people just broke down in tears once they sat down and reflected on the experience."

Because of this incident, Rosa Parks lost her job, as did her husband, because of their political activism. They also received numerous death threats. Nevertheless, they continued to pursue their efforts to eliminate segregation in Alabama. After this harrowing incident, Rosa Parks and her husband moved to Virginia and finally settled in Dearborn, Michigan, outside Detroit. Although Dearborn had a reputation for being progressive, Rosa Parks was critical of the effective segregation of housing and education and poor local services in black neighborhoods. Rosa Parks died a poor woman.

Chapter 21

The Southern Manifesto, March 12, 1956

On March 12, 1956, just ten years after my train ride through the South, a majority of southern senators and representatives joined up in Washington, D.C., to present and publicize the "Southern Manifesto," denouncing the Supreme Court's unanimous decision in Brown v. Board of Education, which two years earlier had invalidated racial segregation in public schools.

The vow to resist racial integration by all lawful means heightened the retaliation that underlay the resistance that was highlighted in the media in 1957– 58 during the crisis over integration at Little Rock's Central High School. It was an effort to galvanize segregationist sentiment among white southerners.

Numerous manifesto backers explained that the Southern Manifesto was designed to transmit strong opposition to Brown to citizens outside the old Confederacy. The manifesto was reprinted in newspapers around the country. The Southern Manifesto drafters insisted that although Brown v. Board of Education prohibited state-sanctioned school segregation, the Brown opinion should not be viewed as requiring public school districts to take affirmative action to achieve integration.

Their interpretation was designed to fill the void created by the court's notoriously vague remedial opinion in 1955 that ordered designation to take place "with all deliberate speed." Black leaders observed with deep regret that the manifesto appeared to have proven itself effective in diminishing the North's appetite for integration.

Although the manifesto's drafters failed to achieve their primary goal of motivating the Supreme Court to reverse Brown v. Board of Education, they largely succeeded in realizing their secondary goal: minimizing the reach of the court's historic decision. Rather than view the Southern Manifesto as the last gasp of a dying regime, it may be more accurate to view it as the first breath of the prevailing order.

To fight against Republican rule, many white southerners joined groups such as the Ku Klux Klan that sought to intimidate blacks and keep them from voting. With the end of Reconstruction and the compromise of 1877, oppression of African Americans became rampant under the Jim Crow laws. It would be more than a century until equality for all races would be seriously propelled forward and until the Civil Rights Act of 1966. The quest for civil rights impacts our society today.

Chapter 22
Sit-In Movement, 1960

On February 1, 1960, four black college students walked up to a whites-only lunch counter at the local Woolworth's store in Greensborough, North Carolina, and asked for coffee. When service was refused, the students, despite threats and intimidation, sat quietly and waited to be served.

No one participated in a sit-in without seriousness of purpose. The instructions were simple: just sit quietly and wait to be served. Often the participants would be jeered at and threatened by local customers. In the event of a physical attack, the student would curl up on the floor as he or she was pelted with food or ketchup. Angry onlookers tried to provoke fights that never came. When the police came to arrest the demonstrators, another line of students would take the vacated seats.

The organizers of the sit-ins believed that if the violence were only on the part of the white community, the world would see the righteousness of their cause. Before the end of the school year, more than fifteen hundred black demonstrators had been arrested. But their sacrifice brought results. Slowly, but surely, restaurants throughout the South began to abandon their policies of segregation.

Demonstrators focused not only on lunch counters but also on parks, beaches, libraries, theaters, museums and other public facilities. In

April 1960, activists who had led these sit-ins were invited to hold a conference at Shaw University at North Carolina.

This conference led to the formation of the Student Non-Violent Coordinating Committee (SNCC). The SNCC took these tactics of nonviolent confrontation further and organized the Freedom Rides. In response to the success of the sit-in movement, dining facilities across the South were being desegregated by the summer of 1960.

Attorney General Robert Kennedy ordered federal marshals to protect future riders. Bowing to political and public pressure, the Interstate Commerce Commission soon banned segregation on interstate means of travel. Progress was slow indeed, but the wall between the races was gradually being eroded.

Chapter 23

Freedom Rides, 1961

During the spring of 1961, while I was in Europe traveling first class Freedom Riders in the U.S. were being beaten viciously for attempting to travel on busses unrestricted. They were simply disobeying segregation signs in the U.S.

When the Freedom Riders stopped along the way, black students used facilities designated for whites, and white riders used facilities designated for blacks. This was such a radical departure from what I had seen when I looked out of my compartment window a bit more than a dozen years before and saw the large COLORED and WHITE signs being obeyed precisely.

Student activists from the Congress of Racial Equality (CORE) launched the Freedom Rides to challenge segregation on interstate buses and bus terminals. Traveling on buses from Washington, D.C., to Jackson, Mississippi, the riders met violent opposition in the Deep South, with extensive media attention, eventually forcing federal intervention. On May 24, 1961, the Freedom Riders continued their rides into Jackson, Mississippi, where they were arrested for "breaching the peace" by failing to obey the "white only signs."

By the end of the summer, more than three hundred had been jailed in Mississippi. Freedom Rides involved travel by civil rights activists on interstate buses into the segregated southern U.S. to test the U.S. Supreme Court decision Boynton v. Virginia, decided December

5, 1960, which ruled that segregation was unconstitutional for passengers engaged in interstate travel. Organized by the *Congress of Racial Equality*, the first *Freedom Ride* of the 1960s left Washington, D.C., on May 4, 1961, and was scheduled to arrive in New Orleans on May 17, 1961.

To capitalize on the momentum of the sit-in movement, the *Student Non-Violent Coordinating Committee* (SNCC) was formed in Raleigh, North Carolina, in April 1960. Over the next few years, the SNCC served as one of the leading forces in the Civil Rights Movement, organizing Freedom Riders through the South in 1961.

Several participants were arrested in the bus station. When the two buses reached Anniston, Alabama, an angry mob slashed the tires of one bus and set it aflame. The riders on the other bus were violently attacked, at the Greyhound Bus Station, knocking John Lewis unconscious with a crate and smashing Life photographer Don Urbrock in the face with his own camera. A dozen men surrounded James Zwerg, a white student from Fisk University, and beat him in the face with a suitcase, knocking out his teeth.

Chapter 24

March on Washington for Jobs and Freedom, August 1963

On behalf of a number of black organizations for social and economic justice, A. Philip Randolph wrote a letter on May 24, 1962, to Secretary Stewart Udall of the Department of the Interior regarding permits for a march culminating at the Lincoln Memorial that fall. Plans for the march were stalled when Udall encouraged the groups to consider the Sylvan Theater at the Washington Monument because of the complications of rerouting traffic and the number of tourists at the Lincoln Memorial.

In March 1963, Randolph telegraphed MLK that plans were under way for a June march "for Negro job rights." He asked for MLK's immediate response. MLK joined Randolph, James Farmer of CORE, and SNCC in calling for such an action later that year, declaring, "Let the black laboring masses speak." After notifying President Kennedy (Kennedy) of their intent, the leaders of the major Civil Rights Organization set the march date for August 28.

The stated goals of the protest included "a comprehensive Civil Rights Bill" that would (1) do away with segregated public accommodations, (2) protect the right to vote, (3) provide a mechanism for seeking redress of violations of constitutional rights, (4) begin a massive public works program to train and place unemployed workers, and (5) seek passage of the *Federal Fair Employment Practices Act* barring discrimination in all areas.

As the summer passed, the list of organizations participating in and sponsoring the event expanded to include the *National Association for the Advancement of Colored People* (NAACP), the *National Urban League*, and the United Auto Workers, among many others. The diversity of those in attendance was reflected in the event's speakers, who included Marian Anderson, Odessa, Joan Baez, Ossie Davis, Ruby Dee, Rabbi Joachim Prinz, A. Philip Randolph, Walter Rather, Bayard Rustin, Roy Wilkins, Whitney Young and John Lewis.

A draft of John Lewis's prepared speech, circulated before the march, was denounced for its militant tone, which charged that the Kennedy administration's proposed Civil Rights Act was "too little and too late" and threatened not only to march in Washington but also to march through the South, through the heart of Dixie, the way the North did in the conclusion of the Civil War.

On August 28, 1963, civil rights leaders conducted a political demonstration held in Washington, D.C., to protest racial discrimination and to show support for major Civil Rights Legislation that was pending in Congress. An interracial assembly of more than two hundred thousand people gathered peaceably in the shadow of the *Lincoln Memorial* to demand equal justice for all citizens under the law.

The crowd was uplifted by the emotional strength and prophetic quality of the address given by MLK, came to be known as the "*I Have a Dream*" *speech*, in which he emphasized his faith that all people, someday, would be brothers and sisters. The rising tide of civil rights agitation greatly influenced national opinion and resulted in the passage of the *Civil Rights Act of 1964.*

After the march, MLK and other civil rights leaders met with Kennedy and Vice President Lyndon B. Johnson at the White House, where they discussed the need for bipartisan support for a Civil Rights Act. Though the bills were not passed before Kennedy's death, the provisions of the *Civil Rights Act of 1964* and the *Voting Right Act* of 1965 reflect the demands of the march.

Chapter 25

The Birmingham Bombing, September 1963

On Sunday, September 15, 1963, *the Sixteenth Street Baptist Church* in Birmingham, Alabama, was bombed during their Sunday school classes by white supremacists—a planned act of terrorism by men who were later identified as members of the Ku Klux Klan. The explosion killed four young African American girls, Addie-Mae age fourteen, Denise McNair, age eleven, Carole Robertson, age fourteen and Cynthia Wesley, age fourteen.

Described by MLK as one of the most vicious and tragic crimes ever perpetrated against humanity, the explosion at the church injured twenty-two others. The *Sixteenth Street Baptist Church* bombing marked a turning point in the U.S. during the Civil Rights Movement and contributed to support for passage of the *Civil Rights Act of 1964.*

In response to the attack and to the *March on Washington for Jobs and Freedom*, liberal members of the House judiciary subcommittee, responsible for the Civil Rights Bill, strengthened the bill that the Kennedy administration had sent to Congress in June, to the displeasure of those who believed it now could not pass.

The movement initially found it hard to recruit supporters, with black citizens reluctant and Birmingham police restrained. Slapped with an injunction to cease the demonstrations, MLK decided to go to jail himself. During his confinement, he penned Letter from Birmingham Jail, an eloquent critique of the white moderate who is more devoted to order than to justice, a work included in many compositions and literature courses.

The breakthrough came when the *Southern Christian Leadership Council* (SCLC) organized thousands of black schoolchildren to march in Birmingham. Police used school buses to arrest the hundreds of children who poured into the streets each day. Lacking jail space, Eugene "Bull" Connor, an ardent segregationist, used dogs and firehoses to disperse them.

Images of vicious dogs and police brutality were emblazoned on the front pages of newspapers and on television screens around the world. MLK grasped the international implications of SCLC's strategy: The nation was battling for the minds and hearts of people in Asia and Africa, and there was going to be no respect for the United States if it continued depriving men and women of the basic rights of life because of the color of their skin.

Kennedy, under pressure, lobbied Birmingham's white business community to reach an agreement. On May 10, 1963, local white business leaders consented to desegregate public facilities, but the details of the accord mattered less than the symbolic triumph. Kennedy pledged to preserve the mediated halt to a spectacle that was seriously damaging the reputation of both Birmingham and the country.

Chapter 26

The Fair Housing Act, 1968

To perpetuate racial segregation, from 1924 to 1950, real estate boards around the country stepped in to institutionalize racial separation. In 1924 the *National Association of Realtor School of Real Estate Brokers* adopted an article in the code of ethics stating that real estate brokers should never be instrumental in introducing into a neighborhood, members of any race or nationality whose presence would clearly be detrimental to property values in that neighborhood, a code that remained in effect until 1950.

After World War II ended, the resulting wave of suburbanization was for whites only. Building on a set of maps originally developed by the *Home-Owners Loan Corporation,* according to credit worthiness, they used the color red to indicate what they considered risky neighborhoods that were ineligible for federally insured loans. Neighborhoods that were black or perceived to be in danger of becoming black were automatically colored red, thus cutting them off from credit and institutionalizing the practice of "redlining."

The *Federal Housing Administration* (FHA) and Veterans Administration (VA) also took a dim view of lending to individual blacks, with the 1939 FHA underwriting manual stating, "If a neighborhood is to retain stability, it is necessary that properties shall continue to be occupied by the same social and racial classes the FHA recommends the use of racially restrictive covenants to ensure and maintain neighborhood stability."

After World War II the massive outflow of whites to the suburbs naturally opened up housing opportunities for blacks in central cities. As urban black populations continued to grow through mass migration, ghetto neighborhoods expanded rapidly in terms of space. By 1970, for the first time, entire cities—Atlanta, Baltimore, Detroit, Gary, Newark and Washington—became majority black.

Many more cities came to house large black pluralities, thus creating a new geography of segregation across municipal as well as neighborhood boundaries, such as in Chicago, Philadelphia, St. Louis, New York and Milwaukee.

In 1937, the *Federal Housing Administration* was authorized to create a mortgage insurance program that would revolutionize housing and lending markets throughout the nation. Provided that the mortgage conformed to criteria established by the FHA, the agency would insure up to 90 percent of a loan's value against default, essentially giving banks a risk-free way of making money.

The conforming criteria increased the geographic concentration of black poverty. The passage of legislation to address housing segregation proved to be among the most difficult tasks undertaken by the Civil Rights Movement. The FHA expressly banned many of the public actions and private practices that had evolved over the years to deny blacks access to housing. It outlawed the refusal to rent or sell to someone because of race, and it prohibited racial discrimination in the terms and conditions of rental loss sales and discrimination in real estate advertising. It banned agents from making untrue statements in order to deny access to blacks, and it enjoined real estate agents from making comments about the race of neighbors or in-movers in order to promote panic selling. Although the new law applied only to around 80 percent of the nation's housing stock, a Supreme Court decision, adjudicated just two months later, extended its reach to all housing in the U.S.

The rapid expansion of black neighborhoods inevitably threatened districts where white elites held place-bound investments. For protection, such white elites turned to urban renewal and public housing programs to block the expansion of black settlement toward imperiled zones. Whenever black residential expansion threatened a favored district, a local urban renewal authority was established to gain control of the land using the power of eminent domain. Black neighborhoods were then razed for "redevelopment" as a middle-class commercial or residential zone. Public housing was constructed in other black neighborhoods to house the displaced black residents, dramatically engaging property owners in a covered area.

Restrictive covenants remained the favorite legal tool institutionalizing segregation, until they were declared unenforceable and contrary to public policy by the *U.S. Supreme Court* in its 1948 decision. Violators could be sued in court for breach of contract. Black outmigration from the rural South continued through the Great Depression and accelerated during the Second World War, reaching peak levels during the 1950s and 1960s. Mass suburbanization in the post-war period was substantially tied to federal policies.

The *Department of Housing and Urban Development* (*HUD*) was authorized only to investigate complaints of housing discrimination and had just thirty days to decide whether to pursue or dismiss allegations. If *HUD* chose to pursue a claim of discrimination, it was empowered only to engage conference, conciliation and persuasion. To resolve the problem, moreover, if the discrimination occurred in a state where there was a substantially equivalent fair housing statute in existence, *HUD* was instructed to hand off the complaint to state authorities. Even if *HUD's* investigation revealed that a victim had suffered blatant discrimination, the agency had no way to enforce compliance, grant a remedy, assess damages, prohibit discriminatory practices from continuing or penalize the lawbreaker in any way.

In the end, the act placed the weight of enforcement largely on the backs of "aggrieved persons" who were granted the right to file a civil suit to recover damages in federal court. The audit likewise indicated the persistence of discrimination against blacks in mortgage lending as well as the continued redlining of black neighborhoods. In recent years, redlining has given way to reverse redlining or predatory lending, in which black borrowers are channeled into high-interest, high-risk loans.

Regardless, as a business model, it is understood that for one to receive a loan, one must be credit worthy regardless of skin color. Just because someone may be disadvantaged does not mean that a financial institution must grant a loan to such a person. That would be bad business. This is what led to the financial meltdown in 2008. Loans were made to people who did not, under normal underwriting practices, have the ability to pay back the debt or failed to read the fine print on their loan documents.

Thus, affordable housing programs carry a considerable load to overcome with the disadvantages of poor minority families because of residential segregation. Recent research indicates that the concentration of neighborhood disadvantage imposed by residential segregation is the leading reason for the perpetuation of black poverty.

Combining greater enforcement of fair housing and fair lending laws with a wider implementation of affordable housing programs would go a long way toward desegregating American society by race and class and moving the nation close to the ideals of the *Fair Housing Act*. Congress made a promise in 1968 that the *Fair Housing Act* has not been able to keep. In nearly fifty years after its passage, the *Fair Housing Act* promise is long overdue.

The housing act is often heralded as a key piece of Civil Rights Legislation, but in reality, it was only the first of several steps Congress undertook to remove residential segregation. It was not until 1977 that Congress passed the *Community Reinvestment Act* to outlaw discrimination against black neighborhoods, thus eliminating the legal basis for the practice of redlining.

I committed myself to the idea that to restrict people because of the color of their skin was immoral. Even before it was declared illegal I found myself challenging all restrictions.

Chapter 27
Moving Forward, 1982–Present

Whenever the economy took a decline, black executives seized upon the opportunity to look elsewhere and believed they might run their own shows and have the good life at the same time. In the late 1980s, during the days of corporate downsizing, many black executives left their corporate jobs because of their frustrations with the hurdles of the corporate world.

After retiring from Xerox in 1982, following my ten years, it seemed to me that corporate America had made a decision to whiten up the corporations again. As a result, there was an increase in the number of blacks leaving corporations and sometimes starting their own businesses. Some left and became consultants at first. Others abandoned all traces of their corporate life, choosing instead to open businesses based on their passions. Many found that the obstacles in the outside world were as harsh as those within corporate America. Because of these obstacles, their ventures often remained small and their start-ups were not strikingly successful. The difference this time around was that the post–civil rights black executives came with stellar credentials.

The post–civil rights generation was propelling the rise in entrepreneurship, particularly for blacks. That is phenomenal. The latest wave of black business growth was vastly different from that of earlier generations. This wave was less common at the neighborhood level of barbershops or family-run funeral homes. The newer entrepreneurs were willing to take risks that twenty years ago blacks were not willing or reasonably able to take. This represents an absolute change in attitude. Blacks no longer felt that the corporate structure was the only way or the safest way for them to rise.

Today's black elites are not likely to seek to be trailblazers as I had been on Wall Street in the 1960's. Access, they felt, is yesterday's battle. Instead, this generation is concerned with what they can accomplish once the door has been pried open. This is also evidenced by the newly acquired success on Wall Street by black billionaires Reginald Lewis in the 1980s and Robert F. Smith decades after the doors of Wall Street were pried open.

Black leaders are saying today, "What does it matter if we can live wherever we want, go anywhere, work anywhere, and play anywhere if we still cannot be comfortable once we get there?" They state that legal segregation, which was highlighted and driven out between 1954 and 1968, did not complete the job. Fortunately, the post–civil rights generation has continued the struggle. But this time, it is from within.

Chapter 28

Black Leaders, 1990s

Black men between the ages of twenty-five and thirty-five with some graduate school experience have started businesses more frequently than any other group in the U.S. As a result, this post–civil rights generation is increasing the number of entrepreneurs for everyone, not just blacks. The black elites have Harvard MBAs and have worked in the nation's biggest companies. Many of the post–civil rights black Wall Street businessmen have better credentials, experience and education today than their counterparts.

This new black elite sees the business world as the connecting link with American power rather than seeing Washington's Capitol Hill as the connecting link. They look to themselves instead of seeking to effect change through government. This generation is marching through freshly opened doors like those pried open on Wall Street by Creative. Rather than fight the power structure head-on, this new generation seeks to seize the power for themselves and to use that power to uplift their entire race. Today's young black professionals have attained the sort of experience, education and connections that those before them could only dream about. They have more potential and see more opportunities than any generation before them. As they rise into circles previously closed to them, they are changing the way the U.S. relates to black America and the way black America relates to the U.S.

In the context of the struggle for civil rights and now equal rights, the new generation has changed their views on race. In earlier generations, many blacks made the choice not to make an issue of race. Today's black elite generation, rather than deny their race in order to be viewed as acceptable, embraces race as a critical component of their professional identity. Instead of downplaying race as an issue, they use race to build a legacy for the next generation of black leaders. They view their success largely as being a result of their refusal to check their blackness at the door.

The blacks in corporate America from this new generation track the shift of the civil rights movement from the streets to the executive suites. They subscribe to the ideology that drives those who are reshaping the U.S. from the top down and from the bottom up. In the years to come, we will see what the consequences of this shift in attitude are and what this will mean for black America and the nation as a whole. This new generation has been successful as never before in the fiercely competitive American mainstream, where race both matters and doesn't matter. At the same time, black executives are struggling with determination to reconcile their collective responsibility to help enable the haves to help the have-nots to become the haves.

Over 50 percent of black wealth to different degrees, diminished in the subprime mortgage crisis of 2008. That should have been avoided with proper financial knowledge. It also should help to raise the bar and lead us to strive for greater collective financial success. Only one generation after slavery ended in the 1860s, self-taught blacks created colleges and universities, thriving businesses and a growing entrepreneurial class of lawyers, doctors, architects, craftsmen, state senators and legislators. This occurred in spite of the fact that at the close of the Civil War in 1865, almost 90 percent of freed slaves were forced to be illiterate because anyone who taught a slave to read or write was subject to incarceration.

PART V
Giving Back, 1950-Present

Chapter 29

Two Improbable Lives and Other Activities

Over many years I have mentored and counseled many young people.

Joe Davis, mentored from 1950–1980

Joe Davis was born and raised in rural Mississippi in the 1940s. When he was growing up, schools were segregated and restricted for blacks. He was in his early twenties and had little schooling when he arrived in New York. After meeting Joe I was able to help him become enrolled in an accredited private school Rhodes in Manhattan with night classes on a full scholarship basis where he was able to earn a high school diploma. While attending Rhodes, Joe worked on a day job as a licensed taxi driver in New York.

One day on my day off, Joe invited me to ride with him as he picked up and dropped off passengers occasionally from the airports. What impressed me most was how thoroughly Joe had learned the streets of five boroughs of New York city in a few months.

A few years later Joe took flying lessons at Teterboro airport in New Jersey. One day off, Joe invited me to come and fly with him and I finally agreed to take him up on it, and we flew over New York city, the Hudson River and New Jersey. I was amazed at Joe's thoroughness and his keen sense of detail. A few years later Joe started an Executive Search Firm business, in Manhattan that specialized in finding specific executive talent for corporations. Joe acquired search assignments for the Ford Foundation and other large corporations.

Our paths crossed again when he got a lead that Xerox Corporation was looking for me after reading an article in *The New York Times* and Joe arranged my visit to the Xerox Corporation for a preliminary meeting when I was on the faculty of Fordham University and was running my own business. I accepted a position at Xerox which lasted ten years.

Joe Davis in our garden

Nicole Clark-Somerville, mentored from 1998—2020

Nicole Clark-Somerville was born and raised in Bridgeport a city in Connecticut, where she completed high school and went to Hampton College, in Virginia, for a year until her money was exhausted. With odd jobs and night school, she earned a bachelor's degree from the University of Bridgeport.

I became Rotary District Governor of Westport Rotary International in 2000, when I met Nicole and became her mentor. Nicole completed her undergraduate degree, at the University of Bridgeport. She worked for a year as a human rights observer for Nisgua Inc., a human rights organization, and went to Guatemala for about a year where she accompanied genocide victims to the Ministerium Publico in the capital city of Guatemala. She documented and reported on her daily activities within her region while in Guatemala and produced bimonthly reports in English and Spanish.

When Nicole returned to Bridgeport, Connecticut, she expressed her conviction that she could not go on to graduate school because of a lack of funds. I convinced her that she should apply for an overseas scholarship and that I would help her with her application. I was able to find a suitable scholarship through Rotary.

Nicole applied and was granted a scholarship to the Christian University in Tokyo with a $63,000 stipend for a master's program. After two years of study in Tokyo, Nicole completed her master's degree. She then became an administrator at a bilingual charter school in Washington, D.C., followed by an administrator position in Benin, Africa., and an administrative position in Connecticut.

Nicole Clark Somerville completes her Masters in Tokyo, Japan University

Win Allen scoring "200" in two bowling games
in the Westport Bowling League

I was active in a series of local sport and recreational activities of which the Bowling League was one. The bowling league met weekly for over two years until the Pandemic curtailed meetings.

PART VI

Rotary Work and Other Projects

Chapter 30

Rotary Work and Other Projects

Rotary Foundation project team in South Africa. Author with wife, Ruby, in center of photo. Team leader, Rotary International Vice President Sonny Brown and wife, Ann, back row, left.

Winston Allen inauguration as Rotary district governor, with Rotary International Vice President Abraham Gordon, 2000.

Governor Winston Allen with Rotary Past District
Governors and senior officials

During my stay as a member of Rotary International since the 1970s, I have volunteered my services for the welfare of others nationally and internationally. Rotary International, founded in 1905, has a membership of one million two hundred thousand whose mission is "service above self."

WESTPORT NEWS, Friday, July 15, 1994

GREAT WALL: The July 23 Great Race, sponsored by the Sunri
Rotary of Westport, got some international exposure recently i
members of the Rotary went to the Great Wall of China near Beiji
and displayed a Great Race T-shirt. Pictured from left to right ar
Winston Allen, Jo Fox, Jo Fuchs and Ruby Allen, all members of t
Rotary. They were attending the Rotary International Conventic
in Taipei, Taiwan.
—Contributed pho

Ruby and Winston Allen in mainland China in 1994

There was a campaign by some relatively few Rotarians to make certain that I would not, although rumored, be selected to become District Governor. This was not surprising to me, because it is but one of the hurdles I have learned to overcome. It nevertheless amazed one of the past District Governors and he shared his behind-the-scene story with me before I became District Governor.

Past District Governor Leask told me this experience he had:

> I was quite surprised when I received a phone call from Mike, a past president of the club that Win was then president of that Win was ignoring the advice of the past presidents and he wanted me to be sure

Win would never ever become District Governor. He wanted me be sure to tell the nominating committee to deny him the votes. I told Mike I couldn't do that because I didn't think it was right and that one person or even a small group of people shouldn't be able to block someone from being a District Governor. He again told me that he did not want me to tell Win about his call.

All Past District Governor's gave Winston an overwhelming vote of confidence and he received one vote short of a unanimous vote and became an acclaimed District Governor who was also elected to serve a second term as Chairman of the Presidents Educational Training Program (PETS).

Prior to my term as District Governor, my wife, Ruby, and I traveled widely throughout the Far East, including to China, Thailand, Malaysia, Indonesia and also to Australia, New Zealand, Mexico, Central America and South America—Guatemala, Chile, Peru, Argentina and Brazil. While I was Rotary District Governor, our travels continued.

WIN with WIN

HELP BUILD A
SHELTER FOR
JEREMIE, HAITI'S
STREET KIDS

I served as a volunteer with a Rotary dental team in the villages of Jérémie, Haiti, to provide free dental services to families with no dental medical care open to them. The lines for the free once a year service was about a mile long and since the dentist was not going to be available for follow-up calls was restricted to extractions only.

While in Jeremie, Haiti, I celebrated the villager's achievement in using the $30,000 I raised for the project in building what I called "happy houses" the cement houses that replaced the thatched-roof huts that prevailed in the towns in 1999.

During my term as District Governor of Rotary International in 2000, I spent a month in South Africa evaluating Rotary programs. While there, Ruby and I witnessed the energy of the people whose volunteers staffed eye clinics, AIDS hostels and the children's hospital in South Africa. Among the self-help programs we visited the Hospice for AIDS Orphans near Johannesburg. Also, we visited Saint John's

Mobile Eye Clinic, which provided eye exams and glasses for the people of the village, and a cerebral palsy rehabilitation clinic in Randburg, Johannesburg.

This followed apartheid and the living conditions during this time were suffering the effects of the struggle to overcome apartheid. We observed a project that provided donated books for the South African schools by Rotary districts in the U.S. In one case, twenty-seven thousand books were donated and received for use by schoolchildren.

We also visited in Cape Town the only children's hospital in sub-Saharan Africa, and a center for deaf children. We visited schools where children were learning in spite of the absence of books and other school materials. Kids were eager to learn. Many of the elementary schoolchildren had to start their six-mile walk to school each day before dawn in order to arrive on time. This happened after apartheid in 2000.

My voluntary work with Rotary was filled with opportunities that I seized upon and that inspired me. Further along the road of giving back, I formed a 501(c)(3) nonprofit organization, the Winston E. Allen Foundation, which continues to this day, with a mission to provide awards to selected students and entrepreneurs.

All Rotary trips were at the volunteer's own expense, as 100 percent of the approximately $70 million raised annually by the Rotary Foundation was used solely for humanitarian projects.

A Winston E. Allen (WEAF) Foundation Meeting

Ruby and I became Rotary Foundation major donors with a contribution of $10,000. Following my term as District Governor, I was elected Chairman of a multistate governing board of District Governors whose mission was to organize the president-elect training of incoming Rotary Club presidents in a seven-district training system (PETS) throughout New England and Canada.

District Governor Win, Ruby and our poodle Joey off on a flight to a Block Island luncheon meeting off the coast of Westport, Connecticut.

Taking Care of Children in Cape-town, South Africa

Winston Allen receives an award as Past District Governor

The Winston E. Allen Foundation (WEAF), a 501(c)(3) nonprofit public foundation. WEAF's aim is to find charitable support for low-income, underrepresented and minority students in college populations, as well as fledging entrepreneurs, seeking to encourage greater awareness of available opportunities.

The mission of WEAF is to serve as a philanthropic nonprofit organization to promote economic empowerment. I also founded the Black Book Club in New York, distributing hundreds of books, largely with black themes and authors, to appreciative purchasers. Regardless of how noble its goals, a public foundation that has a 501(c)(3) tax exemption cannot keep its exemption if it does not serve a public, rather than a private, interest. WEAF has established bylaws, a board of directors, officers and a plan of operation, which includes fundraising.

Reflections

When I reflect on the incredible life I have lived, I recognize that stories like mine help in understanding the impact of Civil Rights and racial animosities in the U.S. It is an important reminder that the days of segregation were not that long ago and although things are slowly changing there is still much work that needs to be done. Learning how I dealt with hurdles and barriers to break into Wall Street is enlightening and the examples of giving back to the community by helping increase wealth, mentoring and founding a non-profit, is inspirational.

As a black in white America, I had challenges that most white people don't have to think about: being locked in a train compartment at thirteen years of age while traveling through difficult areas in the U.S. during the 1940's; being reviled against because I had purchased a house in a red-lined town of Larchmont, New York in Westchester, New York; being denied entry into any Wall Street training program because I was black.

In the early 1960's Wall Street was a citadel of segregation in the U.S. and it was as restricted as the segregated interstate train that I was locked into in the 1940's, without the need for blatant segregation.

When I was told that I could not realize my dream because the door was shut to me, I knew that I was uniquely qualified, and therefore took advantage of a little-known crack in the door for firms and whites only. I seized upon a method for becoming an independent broker-dealer, and became the first black to break the color barrier and enter the front door of Wall Street.

I was subsequently able to open many doors particularly to blacks during the past 60 years. It was an opportunity that I took because I felt it was not likely to come along again. I had to continue working harder in fulfillment of all of my dreams.

If I was in business just to make money, I was in the wrong place. I ran into obstacles, and people stood in my way, but I had to look at what I felt I deserved, and then fight for it. I had to know what I stood for. When I went after what I wanted in my life, opportunities that I could not anticipate, happened to me. I was unique with a plan and I was not going to be merely a copy.

I learned on the job. I had to go at it with all my spirit. I had to live with passion, drive and energy if I wanted to make a difference. Because I stood for something, for integrity and for hard work, I could leave a legacy of success. I had dreams and decided to pursue them. That was what was important.

Appendix

Civil Rights Movement

1955   Emmett Till, a fourteen-year-old, murdered in Mississippi by white racists

1955   Rosa Parks arrested for her refusal to move to the back of the bus

1957   Governor Faubus calls out National Guard to prevent access to Central High School

1961   Sit-ins, nonviolent protests against refusal to be served

1959   Williams debate. NAACP's Robert Williams proposes violence against the Ku Klux Klan

1962   Freedom Riders demand no segregation in interstate travel

University desegregation at southern colleges and universities

Charlayne Hunter

Hamilton Holmes

Albany Movement. Desegregation of entire community; one thousand arrested

1963   Birmingham campaign. SCLC to end segregation and employment

March on Washington. King's "I Have a Dream" speech

Malcolm X advocates black supremacy and rejected racial integration

St. Augustine, Florida, movement practices armed self-defense

Chester School protests. Civil rights demonstration against de facto segregation in the city's eighteen public schools

1964   Freedom Summer. Voting in Mississippi

1964   Civil Rights Act outlaws de jure discrimination and segregation

Harlem riot. Police shoot unarmed black teenager. Riot by black residents

Selma voting rights. Bloody Sunday

Voting Rights Act suspends literacy and other voter registration tests

Watts riots against abuse of blacks

Black Power promotes use of armed self-defense

1968   Fair Housing Act prohibits discrimination in the sale or rental of housing nationwide

Civil Rights Act prohibits discrimination in sales and rental financing based on race, religion, and/or national origin

Assassination of Dr. Martin Luther King Jr.

Sanitation workers' strike

Index

About the Author

Winston E. Allen (Allen), an independent broker-dealer, college professor and Fulbright scholar, is founder and CEO of Creative Investor Services, a multiservice investment firm based in New York City that has been in operation since 1962, to train and bring to the black community unusual investment and career opportunities.

In 1962, when his firm was founded, blacks were restricted from entering the world of Wall Street. Allen, with his Fulbright Scholarship, his Fordham University professorship and his Economics teaching was uniquely qualified to remedy this situation. He plunged right in and overcame the barriers, hurdles and obstacles that he faced in founding the first black-owned independent broker-dealer firm.

Through his contacts he was able to surmount his biggest hurdle, finding personnel. Since Allen found that there was no reservoir of licensed representatives for him to draw from, he quickly decided to recruit, train and begin a drive to find prospects for his company's growth.

He decided to develop and train his own staff, a move that would help additional people gain a foothold in the securities business. His New York operation became a center of recruitment and training, as well as a center for providing an investment service to the local residents who made up a large part of his client base, in addition to his operation out of Westchester, N.Y.

Since the exam given by the National Association of Securities Dealers (NASD) is a difficult one for prospective Series 7 registered representatives, Allen started his people from scratch and taught them the fundamentals. When they finished a one-month crash course and passed the NASD exam, they became salespeople until they became established, at which point they become full-time producers. His graduates were paid very high commissions, and none were lured away by other businesses. His staff of almost a hundred salesmen accounted for more than $3 million in sales in 1969.

Allen managed a dual career as an educator and a licensed broker dealer involved in the securities field. One career strengthened the other. For example, the evaluation he did for the Job Corps in 1960 under the auspices of the Office of Economic Opportunities showed him how many people were working in dead-end jobs, which in turn gave weight to his ideas for Creative Investor Services. Theory and practice did indeed strengthen each other. He founded Creative Investor Services in 1962. When it began to demand more and more of his time, he decided to make a full commitment to the firm in 1964.

A native of New York City, Allen graduated from the prestigious High School of Music and Art. After earning a BA in Economics from New York University, and later a master's degree, he was awarded a Fulbright Scholarship to the University of Paris, the Sorbonne. He then graduated with a Ph.D. from Fordham University.

Allen dearly loves to travel. Ever since his Fulbright days and trips to twenty-five countries, he has traveled to the Middle East, Africa, South America and Central America with Rotary International as District Governor and beyond.

New careers are nothing new to Allen. His interests are vast. He was recruited by Xerox Corporation, where he transformed the company's international training after an article appeared in *The New York Times Business Section* highlighting his success in his training and the CEO recruited him. He taught at the business school at American University and George Washington University graduate schools. He and his wife, Ruby, have resided in Westport, Connecticut, since 1975. A son, Vaughn, is an educator, and a daughter, Julie, is an engineer.

Printed in the United States
by Baker & Taylor Publisher Services